Brian Darwent

BACK TO THE DRAWING BOARD

A memoir of the pre-computer age

First published in paperback by
Michael Terence Publishing in 2024
www.mtp.agency

ISBN 9781800947504

Front cover image
courtesy of Rabecca Ravetto

Michael Terence
Publishing

I think it can be tremendously refreshing if a creator of literature has something on his mind other than a history of literature so far. Literature should not disappear up its own asshole, so to speak.

Kurt Vonnegut
The Last Interview

Contents

TIME WAS...

Oh, I had it easy, let's face it! Forty years as a draughtsman, more or less. Working on a proper drawing board, with pencil and paper. Designing things. Well, mechanical things, admittedly, but so what? Not so many people ever get to design *anything* real. And they even began to call us designers in later years. Nor was the job badly paid - certainly in that late period, when it became easy for me to escape pretty often from the drawing-board shackle. It's a golden rule. The less you do that's useful, the more handsomely you're apt to be rewarded.

Time was when it all looked rather different to me, however - like I might be wasting my life. Maybe I could have been a writer, or artist, or something like that, I used to imagine, instead of labouring at a drawing board. Fat chance, of course.

But what do the young do today? Is life any better for them? Well, the last I heard of it, lots of them were doing very little. No jobs for them, never mind decent jobs. There can't be many big drawing offices left up and down the land for them to find a home in. I suppose you'd have to substitute call centres as some sort of equivalent. There seem to be lots of those, at any rate. I ask you, though, would it be any better working in a call centre than a drawing office? I fancy not.

And do these modern jobs have any *security,* never mind a decent pension scheme? You get the feeling that it's just hire-and-fire these days. Wherever you worked in the old days you felt looked after, at least up to a point. You'd belong to a union. And even medium-sized companies would have a good personnel department and offer a degree of social support. They'd probably have a medical centre, too. With a really *big* firm there might even be a *dentist* on the site. And it was quite rare for anyone to lose their job back then. How young people are supposed to plan their futures now, I don't know. Where once there existed lots of big, seemingly indestructible industrial companies, today there's precious little left that looks permanent. The world is going backwards.

It's all computers these days, too. Sitting at a big, wooden drawing board might not sound like heaven, but is working on a screen any better? And where's the personal satisfaction? If it's a skill, it doesn't seem to leave much of a trace. A printout of some kind, maybe. Technical drawing, as it used to be called, was an art. A minor art, you could say, but still an art. You finished up with something tangible, right there before your eyes. And there was plenty of scope for improving your technique, your aim being to produce drawings in a style instantly recognisable as your own, so that colleagues and others who chanced upon them would know who the draughtsman was without having to check the signature, and perhaps even pause briefly to admire your artistry. It used to take half a lifetime to achieve a style you were finally happy with.

So maybe it wasn't such a *minor* art, after all. Michelangelo must have worked at a drawing board when he was designing the dome of St Peter's. Any drawing that consists chiefly of straight lines, curves and circles would have to be done that way. And Leonardo also had one, I bet, along with tee squares, set squares, compasses and the rest of the paraphernalia. There is definitely a kind of beauty in technical drawings executed with style, even those created by ordinary mortals that don't happen to be architectural. Through to the very end of my working life, in the late 1990s, I never *touched* a computer, but held on grimly to my drawing board. And working on Research and

Development projects, I used to fancy myself as a modern-day Leonardo. There's a great deal of satisfaction to be gained from exercising a manual skill. Computers just don't do it for you.

I suppose there must be *some* drawing offices still left - smaller, at a guess, than in my years, and doubtless full of computer-aided-design equipment. But fancy generating a complex technical drawing with a mouse and keyboard, anyway! To me, it sounds like working with your hands tied behind you. A bit like those kids' toys - where you create a picture on a little plastic screen by turning knobs. I forget what they're called. Must be getting old.

*

But how did I *become* a draughtsman? For most young men in my part of the world it was never more than an aspiration. Jobs in engineering - apprenticeships, that is - were the best thing available if you'd left school without any qualifications, as was quite normal in the 1950s. Then, if you went to night school and got your National Certificate and the rest of it, after at least five years on the shop floor you *might,* if you were extremely lucky, be selected for the Drawing Office. Very few made it.

I was a little different, in as much as I had been to grammar school. But I'd failed to apply myself, and got only three O-levels, as they used to be called, one of them Art. There was no academic way forward, so I left school. I was closer to seventeen than sixteen. What could I do? Almost everybody I knew had got into an apprenticeship. Trouble was, they had strict rules about age. You had to start at *fifteen.* By staying on to take my O' level exams I had ruled myself out. Even in those fairer times, life could still play dirty tricks on you.

Training as a bus conductor looked to be the only option. Then my father went to see the Chief Engineer at *his* firm and pleaded with him to take me on as a kind of mature apprentice draughtsman. Well, by good luck there happened to be a poky little drawing office, tucked far away from mainstream activities, with just such a vacancy. What swung it in the end, I believe, was my O-level in Art. It was virtually unheard of, but I'd be working at a drawing board from my very first day.

The fact was, though, that I had no more idea what a draughtsman did than about engineering in general. Nevertheless, back at grammar school, filling in a form to do with career opportunities, I had answered a question asking what sort of mind I believed I had by writing "mechanical or artistic". The "mechanical" bit wasn't true. I had put that down because I didn't think "artistic" was going to get me very far. In fact I had hit upon exactly the kind of split personality that was generally needed for the job. The people in the local Careers Office had failed to spot it, though. A job in a bank might be suitable, they thought - *if* I could pass the necessary O' levels.

As to the unorthodox career path I was embarking upon, I had no idea if, without the usual shop-floor experience, I would one day be able to pass myself off as a fully-qualified draughtsman. But that was for the future. All that mattered for now was that, thanks to my father, I not only had a job but a *staff* job - even if the starting wage was to be only two pounds ten shillings a week. And with access to the staff canteen, too. My dad had a supervisory role which used to keep him awake at night, but he would never be allowed near the staff canteen. He worked in a brown smock.

Well, the Queen was twenty-nine in that year, Prince Charles only seven… It was 1955… September…

1
JIM MCNULTY AND THE NEW STONE

"Have you brought a *nosebag* with you?" Jim McNulty asked me, on that very first morning at Modern Age Gas Appliances (as I'll call them). Jim ran the poky little drawing office I was to work in. In fact he was its only occupant.

"What?… I'm sorry - pardon?"

A nosebag? Could it be it something rude? I had no idea what he meant and felt my cheeks starting to burn. That used to happen with me when I was only very slightly confused or embarrassed.

"Something for your *lunch?*"

"Oh."

He meant food, I could see, but I was still lost. We'd always called a midday meal *dinner* at home, but I knew that posher people referred to it as lunch, though Jim didn't exactly strike me as posh. And surely I wasn't expected to bring a midday meal with me to work. I'd already been told about the subsidised staff canteen I would be able to use.

"What's in there?" Jim asked, pointing. He had piercing blue eyes.

I nervously patted my canvas shoulder bag - a relic from the war years that had somehow come into my possession.

"Oh, just a few sandwiches," I explained, relieved at last to be able to answer a question. "I thought I'd eat them mid-morning."

"For your *lunch*, then?"

"Oh… er, yes. For lunch. Right."

Having established that I wasn't going to starve, Jim went on to explain how hard it could be to spend the day on your feet when you weren't used to it. Being so much younger than him I thought I would be able to manage, but I wasn't then aware of his curious advantage in the foot department. He wore boots in all seasons, I would later notice, and his feet seemed disproportionately large. After only an hour or two on my own more normal feet I began to understand what he meant.

But the strange thing was that the office did have a solitary chair. I naturally felt that he had first claim to it, but he showed no sign of wishing to sit. And yet, despite his expression of concern, he gave me no hint that the office chair was there for my use as well. It was a situation that would persist throughout our time together. Jim's outsize feet were something he could relax on, no effort of balance or support seemingly being required. I would find myself waiting until he was out of the office before stealing the luxury of sitting down for a minute or two, and even then I'd have a conscience about it.

Jim McNulty was a small, wiry man of around fifty. You could tell that he might once have been quite good-looking, but something had happened. His face was the most deeply lined I have ever encountered. His vivid blue eyes shone out of a Crewe Junction of cracks and crevices. From first sighting I wondered how he managed to shave in a morning. I pictured a technique of stretching the skin across each of the cracks in turn with the fingers of one hand, so that the hairs stood up long enough in daylight to be swiftly scraped away. It was a hazardous procedure by the look of it, for he would often appear in the mornings with bits of tissue paper stuck to his face, stained with blood.

Jim was a heavy smoker, though it wasn't something that bothered me. In 1955, just about everybody smoked. But it did help to explain the layer of dust he seemed to carry around with him. The other cause was his perpetual dandruff. He was losing his hair, and the white flecks could be seen on his scalp as well as his collar. At the front he had an island tuft, embedded in dandruff, which he would hold carefully in place while he combed his other remaining hair. Amongst my teenage fears, I believed I was beginning to go prematurely bald myself, so I took a close interest in other people's hair loss. The individual hairs in Jim's island tuft could have been accurately counted at the time of our first meeting. When I saw him for the last time five years later, the tuft, while a little greyer, would still be hanging on. The business of holding it carefully in place during combing had proved to be surprisingly effective.

*

There had been others in Jim McNulty's small office - or the Maintenance Drawing Office, as it was called - though whether they had been mature apprentices like me I never found out. One by one they had moved on to the main Design Office, but they had not left without trace. The dark-green painted hardboard panelling of the Maintenance Drawing Office had been damaged or broken here and there, with no attempt made to repair it. The legend was that each of my predecessors had been propelled by the playful fists of Harold Major at some point, to leave a distinctive personal imprint. Harold Major was the Chief Engineer, and the man my dad had bravely approached to beg for a job for me. He was Jim's boss.

The poky little office was subterranean. In fact there was a strip of window close to the ceiling through which a little daylight penetrated via a grating above, but fluorescent lighting was needed all day and all year. It made the cracks and hollows in Jim's rugged countenance more starkly visible, while my tendency to blush at the slightest thing had no hope of being concealed.

The most awkward moment of the day came for me when the mail girl called, especially if I was in the office by myself. I was quite terrified of girls. I would try to carry on with my work, but she would invariably have some pointless question to ask, which I couldn't answer without blushing. Usually it was about nothing more provocative than the weather - which was of course invisible to me - but now and again I thought I detected rudeness in the question ("Have you got the time?"), and that made my embarrassment even more acute. It wasn't a comfortable thought, but I used to wonder if the questions were being deliberately concocted in the Mail Room.

Mostly, though, I was remote from and had very little contact with younger people in the firm. And I was kept busy, anyway. The office had acquired, or had inflicted on it, a number of routine tasks, unrelated to its real function, which were carried out by the resident apprentice. These included such time-consuming jobs as reading and recording on a daily or weekly basis various electricity, gas and water meters hidden away in wet or dusty locations all over the large factory. Another, more intricate task involved removing the paper tape from the night watchman's time clock and inserting a new blank one. Consequently there was little time left, in the early days at any rate, for me to learn about the more serious business of producing actual drawings.

And there was another little problem. I had a drawing board of my own, identical to his, but Jim liked doing the drawings *himself*, I began to suspect. New extensions were being planned for the factory, and he had drawn up a number of alternative schemes. These were forever being updated, and for each fresh issue many prints had to be prepared, fully coloured and marked up with a key. This was one of the few proper jobs he seemed willing to trust me with. It took me right back to my days with colouring books as a child. But I would be with him long enough to learn at least the rudiments of technical drawing, and to admire and slowly try to imitate his superb technique.

*

This began quite naturally with sharpening his pencil. Pencils in the 1950s were always wooden, and usually hexagonal in cross section. Using a small and apparently near-useless penknife, Jim McNulty could quickly pare down the most beautifully proportioned pencil business-end you might ever see. The results from a good pencil sharpener can often be satisfying, but in the case of a Jim McNulty crafted pencil you could see the fine knife marks in the wood and know that you were looking at a minor work of art, however transient.

After the shaving of the wood, the exposed pencil lead had to be carefully finished on a piece of sandpaper before it was ready to apply to the drawing paper. By some miracle, Jim could make the same scrap of sandpaper last for weeks. But the real art began with the scribing of lines. The straight lines of a drawing would be done with straight edges - a tee square or set square. And a pencil is after all only a pencil, even when sharpened to perfection. How then could such simple marks seem to have a special quality? Maybe it was in the eye of the beholder. It wasn't simply a matter of neatness. A pencil line, even one drawn with a straight edge, *lives.* And Jim McNulty's straight lines were unmistakably his own.

But as, unobserved, I watched his method unfold, I was most in awe of his printing (or lettering) method. It was an aspect of draughtsmanship that obsessed fledgling draughtsmen, I would learn. For his printing was the main element of a draughtsman's art - the chief means by which he would stamp his authority and personality on his work and thus impress his colleagues and gain a reputation.

At this point of course I had only one colleague. He, however, was a master. Gazing upon Jim McNulty's effortlessly executed printing, which bordered on calligraphy, I realised I was looking at art, or craftsmanship - call it what you will - that I might never equal in a whole working lifetime.

*

It was during my period with Jim that my fear and embarrassment in the presence of girls reached a climax. It was impossible for me to be within *ten yards* of a girl I fancied, without going bright red. But this didn't mean I lost interest in them, and I hadn't been at Modern Age Gas Appliances for long before I fell hopelessly in love with a girl who worked somewhere in the upstairs offices. Her name was Gillian Wade, and it was her *profile* that did it - much to my own astonishment. Profiles have rather gone out of fashion, today's film stars being less concerned about which is their best side than they once were. But from the curve of her brow to the tip of her chin,

Gillian's profile struck me as perfect. And her fair hair, swept off her face and tied at the back, set it off beautifully.

It was surprising that I'd even noticed Gillian, however, never mind learnt her name, because our paths seldom crossed. Nor did I try to get any closer. My combination of fear and infatuation in fact kept me as far away from the girl as possible, and it wouldn't have surprised me to know that she was unaware of my existence.

Why did some people blush? I asked myself over and over. And why was I such a bad case? I could see the advantages of going red in the face if you were in angry confrontation with an enemy, but what earthly use was it in relations with the opposite sex? It got you noticed, it was true, but hardly in a way you would want. It was *awful.*

Although Gillian and I didn't come into anything like contact in the working day, there was nevertheless a time of danger, for we both used the staff canteen. I would go to extraordinary lengths to avoid being next to her - or in fact anywhere *near* her - in the self-service queue. But a day inevitably came when I was not careful enough - and suddenly there she was, directly behind me. I very nearly fled from the place, but somehow I managed to hang on - without so much as glancing at the girl, of course, after my first moment of shocked surprise - until my turn at last came to be served.

Having collected my lunch, I was able to move away just a little to where the knives and forks were. I hoped to get away altogether without further delay, but someone was blocking my way. In my desperate haste I grabbed my eating irons, then swung around in the other direction - and our trays collided. Mine fell from my trembling fingers. Turning instantly red, I spluttered an apology, then bent down to try to retrieve my lunch - which at least put me out of general sight. But my ordeal wasn't over. To add to my embarrassment, Gillian put her tray on a convenient table and got down with me. We had a private moment together, surveying the terrible mess on the tiles. Then she too became embarrassed, and left me to it. The meal was a write-off, anyway. One of the dinner ladies came forward to tell me someone would clean it all up, and to offer me a replacement meal, but I declined, preferring a swift exit. I didn't dare go back in there for weeks. Instead, I walked half a mile each day to a fish-and-chip shop.

One day, soon after the canteen incident, I was walking through the office reception area when I almost bumped into Gillian Wade. She was deep in conversation with another girl, whom I recognised as one of the mail girls. I did a quick sidestep, and was about to disappear through a convenient door when I distinctly heard the other girl say:

"Go on - ask him now!"

"Ask me what?" I managed to enquire, before my inevitable attack of blushing had had time to overwhelm me.

But the two girls only giggled, then ran off - Gillian herself blushing a little, I noticed - up a flight of stairs. I stumbled back to Jim McNulty's dusty underground lair in a state of shock and confusion.

But I never did find out what her question was. She wasn't inclined to follow the matter up, apparently, even via her friend. Too scared even to think of approaching her directly, I told myself that it was probably just another of the silly questions the mail girls were still sometimes asking me. And then Gillian

Wade abruptly left Modern Age while I was still wrestling with the matter, and that was that.

*

Jim's contentment with the drawing equipment in his office was a puzzle to me. Discarded on top of a tall cupboard was an apparent tangle of junk, which I was slow to realise was actually a draughting machine. This was a device that could be attached to a drawing board. Mounted on it were special scale rules, permanently set at right angles to each other, which also served as straight edges. Governed by an ingenious system of jointed parallel arms, they could be moved quickly and easily all over the drawing surface. I often had to visit the Design Office for blueprints, and was fascinated by just such a device I'd seen in use there, recognising at once that it would take a great deal of the labour out of the job.

With an ordinary drawing board, you see, you had to manipulate a tee-square, set-square and scale rule before you ever got to draw a line with your pencil. The loose scale rule was a particular nuisance. You could either keep picking it up and putting it down, as needed, or else hold it more conveniently between your teeth. On top of that, the type of tee-square Jim was content to use fell off if you tilted the board to a steep enough angle for comfort. And then the triangular set-square was forever slipping underneath the tee-square, so that you had to be pretty dexterous, with your left hand holding the tee-square against the edge of the board, your right holding your pencil, and the scale rule clamped for the moment between your teeth, to catch the thing before it clattered to the floor. A draughting machine would bring everything instantly and securely into play, by contrast, regardless of the tilted angle of the board. The advantage was overwhelmingly obvious to me.

And yet Jim spoke of the tangled machine with strange bitterness, as if it was some new-fangled device that had been invented to rob him of his livelihood, when I raised the matter, and absolutely refused to let me lift it down to have a closer look. The scale rules were lost, anyway, he explained petulantly. It was a curious blind spot that I would never be able to fathom. A good many years would have to pass before I finally had the enormous satisfaction of sitting down at a drawing board with a draughting machine attached.

But producing engineering drawings in that office could sometimes seem like a minor activity. Jim's greatest talent, I noticed, as the months passed, was doing illuminated inscriptions in the front of wedding albums. People brought them to him from all over the factory, and beyond. His major capitals were almost as elaborate as those executed by medieval monks. And on occasion, too, he did very fine pen-and-ink landscape drawings, copied from photographs - all in works' time. These were usually a present for a spouse or relative, though I don't believe he ever charged anyone. He kept a special collection of pens in a drawer for these tasks, and on one occasion I got into serious trouble for damaging the nib of a particular favourite I'd borrowed for some cruder purpose.

Long after I had moved on from Jim's office I would learn that he had never had a technical education or any formal training to speak of, but had manoeuvred himself into the job during the war, picking up the skills as he went along.

*

One day towards the end of my time in the Maintenance Drawing Office Harold Major burst in, thumped the counter - it was a little like a shop, with a lift-up flap - and roared something to the effect that a new stone had to be erected near the Tool Room - would Jim look into it and start to draw up a scheme?

"It could be a job for young Brian," he added. As usual, he didn't hang around after giving his instructions.

"A new *stone*?" I enquired, as the door slammed.

"He means a *piss* stone," Jim explained. "A *urinal*... Would you like to have a go at it?" job.

"But I've never done anything like that."

"Well, I'm very busy just now..."

I must have looked a bit anxious. It would be my first serious design.

"There's no need to worry," he said with a little chuckle. "It'll only be a matter of allowing for big uns and little uns!"

The layout of the site turned out to be such that a urinal of more or less any shape could be fitted in, but the essential choice came down to either a square or rectangular plan. I preferred the square option, which would allow all four walls to be brought at least partly into use. A single access point, with inner screening wall, would be all that was needed for both entrance and exit, I decided. This could be situated at one corner. At the remaining three the man relieving himself would be able to place his feet diagonally, so as to point directly into the corner. This dealt neatly, I reasoned - not without a little smirk - with the matter of accommodating the big uns, three special positions being more than enough, despite all the bragging that went on.

I indicated the dividers according to these ideas on my plan, but Jim McNulty shook his head slowly when he saw it.

"I'd better have a go myself," he sighed, without explanation. "Finish yours off, though, if you like."

Jim didn't begin his scheme until a day or two later, so that I had a head start. When I was finally able to sneak a look at it I saw that he had gone for the rectangular plan, with access from both ends and the stalls arranged along one wall only. I counted them, and saw that five more men could be accommodated in my scheme for a similar floor area. But he admittedly had both an entrance and an exit.

It wasn't long before Harold Major demanded to see how I'd got on. I tentatively showed him my scheme, while Jim remained engrossed in his own work a few steps away.

"Hmm... very good," he said. "I like this corner idea. That's where I would stand... What about the single access, though?"
"I can't see that it's very important," I murmured.

"What do *you* think, Jim?" Mr Major called over his shoulder.

"I'm a bit worried about that combined entrance and exit myself," Jim answered, quickly coming over. said:

"Have you done an alternative scheme?"

"Yes, I dashed something off the other day."

"Well, let's have a look at it!"

The Chief Engineer studied Jim's scheme for a moment or two, then said:

"I see you've labelled one end 'Entrance' and the other 'Exit'. How would they know?"

"They wouldn't, necessarily..."

"You could put up signs, I suppose," laughed Mr Major, looking over the tops of his horn-rimmed glasses into Jim's blue eyes.

"Oh, I don't think that would be needed. I simply thought it would be a good idea for those going in not to have to fight their way through the men just leaving. Enough time is wasted in this factory already."

"But how could they choose the right way to go in without signs?"

Jim shrugged.

"So we'd put up *signs*, then."

"But would the men take any *notice*, do you think?"

"Maybe not..."

Mr Major rather pointedly counted the number of stalls in the rival plans.

"I think young Brian's has it," he announced with finality, giving me a weighty thump on the back. "All this stuff about entrances and exits is a lot of nonsense, if you ask me. I know they're a lazy lot here, but they don't spend all day pissing. Pissing *about*, maybe. I doubt very much if you'll see more than two or three men in here at any one time, in reality. No, we'll go for the square plan... Get on to Gordon's, the builders, and have their man here first thing in the morning. We've been pissing about with this job for long enough."

*

It didn't take Jim very long - no more than the rest of the morning, anyway - to regain his composure. He was really a very good-natured man whose confidence in his own great, if somewhat specialised, talents wasn't easily shaken. But I did enjoy that one small victory over him before leaving the Maintenance Drawing Office - even if it wasn't the kind of victory I could easily brag about to anybody. Least of all to the mail girls!

2
THE BELT MENDER IN WINTER

One Monday morning, a few weeks after my urinal triumph, I carried my few work possessions - consisting mainly of drawing instruments and books needed for my day-release technical-college studies - from Jim McNulty's subterranean den to the Design Office, crossing the Assembly Department and making my way nervously between lines of noisy, whirring machines in the Drilling Shop. On my way I must have passed the workplace of the belt mender, though he was a figure who didn't yet stand out. Emerging into daylight, I crossed the internal factory street and quietly entered my new home.

The door was central, at the top end of a long, brightly-lit office with two rows of drawing boards. Every head was briefly raised as I made my sheepish entrance, but no word was spoken. From the visits I had made for prints, I knew that the Design Office was a place of silence. Down at the far end was a glazed internal office, occupied by Mr Parish, the Chief Draughtsman, to whom I was to report. I had never spoken to him until this day, though I had seen him at a distance, berating some delinquent youth, perhaps - the office employed a large number of apprentices - or standing erect in his office, watching for signs of incipient misbehaviour. Everyone else wore a white smock coat, but Mr Parish had a rather natty off-white jacket. His hands were usually in the pockets, though with the thumbs exposed. When the thumbs were inactive you could relax a little, I would soon learn, but when they began to twitch you had to be on your guard. He had a past reputation for suddenly tearing a drawing which displeased him from the board to which it was pinned, before the poor young draughtsman's startled eyes.

My arrival in the Design Office was a formality, so Parish wasted little time before handing me over to his No 2, the pipe-smoking and grumbling but grandly named Roland Spencer - a bitter man whose embitterment, I would discover, sprang chiefly from Parish's frequent interruptions, at just the moment when he was trying to deal with something important. It was he who ran the office. Parish, now fairly close to retirement, had become only a figurehead. He was quite out of touch with day-to-day matters, but no one had explained this to him, so that, standing in his accustomed spot in his office, random ideas would float into his mind, whereupon he would shout for Mr Spencer before they floated out again. With his eye on the Chief Draughtsman's job, Spencer would be compelled to turn his mind from whatever was engaging it to deal instantly with - and if possible smother - Parish's latest meddling proposal. And always with a forced smile. His normal scowl was invariably directed away from his superior. But all that, as I say, I would find out later.

*

I was given a recently vacated drawing board up at the top end of the office, well away from the serpent gaze of Mr Parish and the sarcasms of Mr Spencer, whose desk and drawing board were of course right next to the Chief Draughtsman's office. Spencer had one of the office's two draughting machines, though he seldom used it, which seemed to me a terrible waste. But I now had a tee-square with a push-button clamp device which held it in place when not in use, and had recently bought a fancy adjustable set-square, which allowed me to draw lines at any angle without having to fiddle with a schoolboy's protractor. I had my own undisputed chair at last, too, and felt well enough equipped as I sat on it, awaiting instructions.

I even felt a little excited. This was the *Design* Office, after all, where the most interesting work was surely done. I wasn't expecting to be asked to design a full gas cooking range for an industrial canteen, but I thought I was bound be given something more stimulating than a urinal to get my teeth into.

It wasn't long before Roland Spencer appeared at my shoulder.

"I want you to start by copying this," he said, handing me a printed sheet covered in letters, numbers and fractions of an inch.

"Oh," I said, puzzled. "Just once, do you mean?"

"Until you get it right."

I scratched my head, deliberately.

"I don't think I'm likely to make any mistakes," I assured him. "I can be very careful."

"Yes, I'm sure you can."

Now I was really mystified.

"So what's it for, then?" I asked.

"You'll need to learn how to print properly."

"What? But I can do that already," I protested. "I've been with Jim McNulty for eighteen months, you know."

"So what does that prove?"

"Well, *his* printing is absolutely brilliant… I think he's a bit of a genius, to be honest."

"*Do* you now?" He grinned for half a second. "And what's that got to do with it?"

"Well, *my* printing isn't bad, either. Have a look."

I'd brought a roll with me of bits of work I'd done with Jim. I slipped off the elastic band and tried to show them to him, to prove that I wasn't a complete novice. He brushed them aside.

'This is how we do things here," he insisted, stabbing at the printed sheet with his finger. It was done by hand, I could see - neatly enough, but in a plain, workmanlike style, entirely devoid of flair. "You're to keep copying this out until I'm satisfied. Got it?"

"But for how *long?"*

"It will take you about a month, if we're to get all that Jim McNulty nonsense out of your head."

*

I was left practically speechless - which was perhaps as well, for I'd heard that Parish and Spencer's favoured method of dealing with dissidents was to subject them to close interrogation in the Chief Draughtsman's office, with a good many hints that they were exceedingly lucky to be working in a drawing office when a shop-floor apprenticeship would plainly be more suitable.

But I was hardly a *serious* rebel. In those days any questioning of instructions - never mind offering ideas or suggestions of one's own – was seen as an open insult to the man who was *paid* to do the thinking, and all this was so ingrained that you accepted it without protest. Only years later would I come to realise just how painfully inefficient that office was, in spite of its culture of unquestioning obedience.

There was always the draughting-machine issue, but take also the sheets of paper (or parchment, as it was called) on which you did your drawings. Anyone at all familiar with engineering drawings will be aware that the border areas are occupied by technical notes, columns listing modifications, boxes for the title, drawing number, draughtsman's initials, scale, date, and so on, even down to the company's name and address -which would usually incorporate (as at Modern Age) a fancy logo. You would expect all this to be already in place on a pre-printed sheet, cut to size.

Well, in this office (it was the same in Jim McNulty's) you had to cut a piece of paper precisely to size from a roll, then, before you could even begin your drawing, laboriously fill in the standard border in pencil. For a large drawing it could take the best part of an hour. As for the company's logo, that, for the not-so-artistic, could add a further fifteen minutes to this futile preparatory work. If you were, say, detailing a simple component on a small-size sheet, the border could often take you longer to do than the drawing itself.

I suppose the truth was that in those days efficiency wasn't seen as desperately important. There wouldn't have been much competition in the home market, with manufacturing still in the process of getting off the ground again after the disruption of the war years, while later overseas competitor nations like Germany and Japan had faced a greater task in rebuilding their industrial base and weren't yet much of a threat. Held to be of far greater importance than real efficiency was the discipline of spending the full number of hours at the drawing board, with minimum time for tea breaks and none at all for private chatting. Most important of all, though, was to be on time in the mornings. Mr Parish used to take up a position outside the office door as half-past eight approached, to encourage stragglers.

"Brian Darwent, you're late again!" he would shout, whereupon I would feel obliged to break into a grudging trot.

*

After Gillian Wade left the company, I never again knew quite the same feeling of panic in the proximity of a girl I fancied, and my life was made easier in the Design Office when mail girls called because of the presence of others. But I had to face another ordeal involving females which was more terrifying than anything experienced before or since.

The bulkier mail generated by the office - chiefly large numbers of prints (folding them in a precise way was a job in itself) - was too heavy for the mail girls to carry. Instead, the younger apprentices had to deliver it, on a rota system, and one of the departments on the list was the Machine Shop.

This frightening place was full of powerful women in green overalls with the sleeves rolled up - on piece work, churning out great heaps of brass components on capstan lathes. It was said that several young men on this mission had been carried off by these amazons to their rest room - strictly women only - and there stripped of their lower garments to have unspeakable things done to their private parts. One or two of the better-looking youths had failed ever to emerge, it was further rumoured, and were still kept under lock-and-key for use on hot afternoons, when lustful passions overcame the drive to achieve the maximum bonus.

The Machine Shop was L-shaped, with a narrow gangway between two rows of lathes. The way-in was on the shorter leg, while the office to which the mail had to be delivered was right at the end of the longer one. No bypass existed. The only way of reaching the office was by making that long, tremulous walk between the two lines of busy but watchful women. I have no clear memory of my first mail delivery. I seemed to float along in a dream. But I know from later experience that from the moment of entry, whistles and catcalls would begin - half-hearted at first, then, when the corner had been turned and the longer leg reached, the animal noises would rise steadily in pitch, to be supplemented finally by the banging of metal implements, and even sometimes the stamping of feet. All this seemed to operate in reverse on the return journey. Once I was safely out of the place I would feel tremendous relief, mingled with a slight disappointment that the ladies had not apparently thought me worth kidnapping.

*

It didn't take me long to see that Roland Spencer had an ideal underling on whom he could vent his embitterment. His victim was a leathery little man with crinkly hair, named Bill Collins. Bill was well into his fifties, but he cycled ten miles to work each day, in all seasons, which was the probable cause of his weathered look. He worked up at the top end of the office, surrounded by apprentices, whom he supervised. In spite of this, he also sought to be on friendly and familiar terms with them.

I joined Bill's squad myself - once Roland Spencer had accepted that I had achieved a satisfactory standard of printing. But I was on the fringes, and feeling a little out of my depth in the early days. I also spent as part of my training a rather aimless period hanging around in various departments "on the works" - they mercifully didn't include the Machine Shop - to gain a little shop-floor experience. So some time elapsed before I was comfortably settled in the Design Office and had become an alert and accepted part of the scene. It was only then that I began to notice the whispered conversations that went on around this man.

Bill Collins' life wasn't easy. He liked to think of himself as the hero of his young friends, but his self-image was forever being undermined by Spencer, who would call for and expect his immediate attention, much as he in turn had to respond to Parish. But what made it worse was that Spencer's commands to him had to be shouted the length of the office - breaking the silence in a very unsettling way. In trying to rise above this rough treatment, and keep the respect and hopefully the admiration of the apprentices, Bill had taken to romancing about his private activities and personal history.

Two of my contemporaries in particular, Des Ramsey and Dave Green, quite obviously delighted in egging Bill on in these flights of his imagination. Both were highly prone to adolescent fits of giggling and convulsive laughter, though Des had less control in that respect. Dave could be surprisingly poker-faced when he was in the mood and usually took the lead.

Bill didn't readily launch into his outlandish tales. They had to be coaxed from him in short, whispered instalments. A freer narration would have been impossible, anyway, because of the need to appear at all times to be hard at work. Even Des seldom broke down completely. All that could probably be seen from Parish and Spencer's end of the office most of the time would be the slight shaking of a pair of shoulders, or the loud blowing of a nose. Only when things got really hysterical did one or other of them have to make a dash for the concealment of the toilet, thankfully only a short distance away. Bill never seemed to notice any of this.

The details of Bill's stories only reached me slowly. At first I didn't altogether disbelieve that he had been the co-designer of the Sherman Tank, or that he was currently the Chief Scout for a leading rugby league club. And since I was unfamiliar with the origins of many of the older popular songs, I could give credence to his claim that in his one-time role as a music-hall impresario and occasional stage performer he had introduced "Lily of Laguna" to Lancashire audiences. One thing I was pretty knowledgeable about, though, was opera singers and operatic arias (this was entirely due to the influence of the popular tenor and film star of the time, Mario Lanza}, and one afternoon, when the whispered conversations somehow turned to the topic of serious music, I asked Bill what he thought of Jussi Bjorling (the Swedish tenor).

"Oh yes, that's a very fine piece," he answered, without a moment's hesitation.

I said nothing to the others, but my regard for Bill Collins' truthfulness was never quite the same after that.

*

So what was I learning, meanwhile? Well, I was moving on beyond the basics of engineering drawing now, certainly. A persistent worry, though, was that the technical subjects I was doing at college seemed to have little connection with stuff we designed at Modern Age. Our technology, in truth, was very ordinary. The products comprised simple iron castings, sheet-metal pressings, brasswork and nuts and bolts. Nor was the pace of change very rapid. Some of our designs for ranges, boilers and other equipment had been around since before the war.

Even so, there always seemed to be plenty to do - or at any rate it was somehow possible to keep an office of twenty people apparently busy. Besides all the laborious border work I've mentioned, every single drawing had to be painstakingly traced in Indian ink onto blue tracing cloth (Irish linen) to make a permanent copy. This was a skilful, but slow business which provided the apprentices - who had first to master the technique, of course - with an endless supply of work. Many drawing offices employed female tracers for this task. (It was a line of work that would soon be overtaken by advances in technology, sad to say: the traditional parchment drawing paper was first superseded by the more durable "melinex" film, and then storage by micro-filming came along.)

Time was also occupied at Modern Age in writing out - in Indian ink on cloth again - long material lists, tooling schedules and such. It would all be rapidly taken care of on a computer by a technical clerk today.

In addition, the younger apprentices had other routine tasks to keep them occupied. Coffee machines were still unknown (or rare), so there was tea to be brewed and washing-up to be done. I recall, also, that we dusted the lampshades and washed the windows on the inside once a month.

We had radiators and steam heating, though, so there were no coal fires to be attended to (part of the morning ritual in earlier drawing offices, I'd heard).

Nevertheless, I did have time to learn how to draw. This was largely a matter of practice and experience. The ability to visualise a component or an assembly in different views, and sometimes in cross section, doesn't come easily, and this had to be married to the skill of constructing what one had visualised on paper, properly to scale and with due allowance for dimensioning and other added information.

Whether the process is helped or hindered working on a screen with modern computer-aided design equipment, I couldn't say. It's true that with sophisticated packages an object can be rotated on the screen, to allow viewing from a variety of angles, but the object has to be defined first. At New Age we learned those skills the old way, but there was still a worry that young draughtsmen elsewhere were being trained in more technical, higher grade work. An apprentice who had spent four years, as I did, under the distant gaze of Mr Parish, his work scrutinised on sudden impulses by Roland Spencer, would emerge second-to-none regarding quality of execution - and with a habit of punctuality as a bonus. But he would carry a deep anxiety in his soul that would take ages to overcome: *he would believe he did not know how to do real engineering.*

*

Upstairs was the office's printing machine. This bore no resemblance to printing equipment today. It was noisy and primitive. Drawings - done essentially on tracing paper - were placed on top of sensitised printing paper and fed into the jaws of the machine. Meanwhile, a carbon-arc lamp, partially visible but too bright to look at, trundled noisily to and fro. It was definitely a piece of mechanical rather than electronic equipment - with a belt drive. Quite frequently this belt would come apart at the join and have to be taken for repair. It was a skilled job requiring the services of a belt mender.

There was only one. His workplace was against a whitewashed wall half way down the Drilling Shop - just across the street from our office. (I'd walked the length of it on my first morning.) It was a spot he had probably occupied for a long time, for the machines in the department had once been belt-driven from overhead line-shafting. By the late 1950s, however, new machines had been installed with their own electric motors. This had happened with machinery of one sort or another throughout the factory, and beyond. So the craft of belt mending was in decline. In fact with the exception of this solitary exponent of the trade, it was virtually extinct.

And another dramatic change was underway in the works, for Jim McNulty's plans for factory reorganisation and extension were starting to be implemented. Several departments, including the Drilling Shop, were scheduled to be transferred to a new green-field site. It was intended that the large vacated space would eventually be occupied by a small subsidiary company at present based on the other side of town, although the timing of this last stage of the plan was very uncertain.

Familiar as I had been - from all the colouring of prints I'd done for Jim - with the details of these changes, I couldn't remember any thought being given to this belt mender in the complex scheme of relocation. I hadn't even known he existed. But now, as the work proceeded, he was becoming increasingly noticeable - generally leaning immobile against the vice mounted at one end of his bench. Evidently the man and his declining trade had been overlooked.

One of the apprentices of course had to take the printing-machine belt for repair, though for some forgotten reason I was never given the job. When I passed the man at a distance, however, I could see that the belt mender was a large. red-faced man in clean blue overalls, with a cap on his head in all seasons. From the fringe of silver hair at the back you would guess that he was probably in his early sixties.

Until recently it hadn't seriously been expected that he would give our little job his immediate attention. With all the activity going on around him it would be assumed that the man was busy. Now, though, when it was becoming very obvious that he was no longer exactly fully stretched, the apprentice on the mission quite naturally felt it was unreasonable that he would have to make a return journey - and more to the point, that the printing machine would have to remain out of action in the meantime. If he ventured to express his impatience, however, it would be to no avail. Regardless of the time of day, the man would have a ready answer:

"I'll see to it after tea break."

*

Meanwhile, discipline up at the top end of the Design Office was showing signs of breaking down. With retirement now no more than a year or two away, Parish was no longer as alert or motivated as he had once been, while Spencer, though still fierce, was too busy to pay much attention. I myself was a factor in the deterioration, too. Despite a certain shyness, I was by nature pretty Bolshie. And I could certainly laugh. In that regard

I was quite the equal of Des Ramsey and Dave Brown. And there was no end to Bill Collins' claims to past and present importance.

One year Des and Dave volunteered, for some reason, to join the works' Entertainments Committee. The main function of this body was to organise an annual Christmas concert for pensioners, to be held in the staff canteen. The talent was to be very much of the amateur kind, but traditionally there would be a "star turn" - someone who had performed in the clubs, at least, and had a modest following.

They weren't inclined to talk about their work on the committee. Bill Collins, however, because of his past experience of the music-hall game, began to pester them about their choice. With limited funds, it happened that the committee was having difficulty finding a suitable star, so Des and Dave had to stall for a while. Bill then began to disparage their efforts. He also began dropping large hints that the committee would benefit greatly from having someone older and more experienced in the team. In fact he *had* helped in the past, but this year he'd been passed-over in favour of new blood. It rankled.

At last they could stand his scorn no longer. With no star turn yet in sight they one day found themselves, without prior collusion, *inventing* one.

"Come on, tell us who you've got for this concert?" Bill asked for the umpteenth time.

"No one, yet," said Des. 'Though we've got a few ideas... Haven't we, Dave?"

"What?... Oh, a few ideas, yes... Well, *one* idea actually."

"Who's that, then?" asked Bill.

The two apprentices looked at each other, reading one another's mind.

"We've got this comedian, you see," said one.

"A comedian," said Bill scornfully. "How original!"

"Well, he isn't just a comedian, of course."

"So, what else does he do?"

"Oh, things… you know."

"Like what?"

'Well… he roller skates."

"Roller skates? Whoever heard of a skating comedian?"

'That's what we thought, but it seems he does… And that isn't all. He does other stuff, too."

"You mean as well as skating?"

'That's right… It seems he *juggles* as well." "After he's finished telling jokes and skating?"

"Well, no. He does it all at the same time. That's his *speciality,* you see."

Bill was silent for a moment, as if searching his memory. I fancy he lit a cigarette at this point. Des, meanwhile, was showing signs of losing control, but Dave was still managing to keep a straight face.

"And even *that* isn't all," he said. "He jumps over things, and goes under tables and through hoops - still on roller skates, still juggling and still telling jokes. He's brilliant!"

Bill looked ready to pounce now.

"What's his name?" he asked, drawing on his cigarette.

Dave held back for a few tantalising seconds.

"Alf Rowley."

"Not *him!"* cried Bill. "I *thought* as much… I remember when he first started. At the old Hippodrome, it was. I introduced him myself, if I remember rightly. *Hopeless,* he was… "

But the poor man was talking to himself by now. Knocking over chairs in their haste, guffaws escaping like stream from a boiler, Des and Dave had dashed for the toilet. Slightly detached, though also convulsed, I was left to face the music when old Parish came hurrying breathlessly up the office to see what all the commotion was about.

There followed an attempt by Parish and Spencer, using their traditional method, to restore order at the top end of the Design Office. The three of us were invited separately into the Chief Draughtsman's office for interview. But we had all experienced these menacing chats before and were becoming immune.

And besides, the changing social climate was against them. These years were the late 1950s. Rock 'n' roll had arrived: first Bill Haley and *Rock Around the Clock,* then Elvis and *Heartbreak Hotel,* then the home-grown products. James Dean had been killed in a car crash, but his image from *Rebel Without a Cause* was everywhere. In a word, teenage rebellion was in the air, and even our factory office with its rigid code of discipline couldn't escape entirely. We had to laugh, at least. In fact laughter was the only direction our rebellion could take. We weren't about to start singing rock 'n' roll songs at the tops of our voices. And so it continued, barely suppressed now, our attention turning away from Bill Collins, who had become uncharacteristically subdued, and increasingly towards the belt mender.

*

With the emptying of the Drilling Shop and the other busy departments that had once surrounded him, the belt mender and his work bench finally stood alone. He could be glimpsed in the distance from the ever- open doorway across the street from the Design Office, always leaning against his vice.

Or at any rate the man could be seen while there was still enough daylight, for the lighting and heating had by now been disconnected. Our interest in this neglected worker intensified in the mid-winter months, when we realised a moment would come in the late afternoon when he would be lost to view. The question then - almost a philosophical one - was whether the belt mender in such circumstances stayed at his post, or sneaked off to find somewhere warmer.

There was of course only one way of finding out - we had to go and see. And so we would start to feel restless as darkness began to fall, and experience a strong urge to sneak out into the street and peer into the gloomy depths. Soon these little excursions became very frequent, in an effort to fix the precise moment when the belt mender disappeared. Usually, upon re-entering, the scout would be incapable of speech, so that the essential fact could only be communicated by a nod or shake of the head. Don't ask me why we found the poor man's predicament so very funny. It strikes me as almost tragic now. But in that controlled environment *everything* seemed funny. We were like giggling schoolboys again. For a time I believe we even kept a wall chart, on which the key moment was plotted in conjunction with weather details and the official sunset time.

And of course our interest didn't end with his disappearance. Once he had gone the scout would feel compelled to enter the gloomy depths, to check on the man at closer range. It must be said as well that in most cases he was discovered to be still immobile at his bench.

Because I had never seen the belt mender or his work bench close up, I was sometimes tempted to do a detour through the old Drilling Shop when out on some errand. I wanted to get as close as I dared, so that I'd be able report back to the others on his amazing lack of activity in exact detail.

One particularly cold afternoon, not long before dusk, I saw to my astonishment that the man was not in his accustomed spot. This was an opportunity, I quickly realised, for me to have a good look at everything. I walked over and stood in front of his bench, trying to imprint the scene on my mind. I even began to make a kind of silent speech, commenting on what I could see: a clutter of strange tools, small tins of this and that, random lengths of belting. Next I tried standing as he normally stood, leaning against the vice.

Suddenly I heard a noise. I turned and was shocked to see that the belt mender was actually present. He had allowed himself the luxury of reclining on a makeshift seat, or bed, half hidden around the end of his work bench, and had made even less visible by the layers of old sacking he had covered himself with against the cold. I was set to make a run for it- but then I saw there was no need. The noise I had heard was a gentle snoring. The belt mender appeared to have hibernated.

3

GREASERS, LIONS AND DUTY-MEN

I had an unusually quiet voice in my younger days (still do have), so that unless I made an effort I could be misheard or misunderstood. Perhaps not even heard at all. I suffered especially when speaking to strangers in shops and other places, across counters. But I also had a peculiar gift for getting at cross purposes with people even when I *did* raise my voice. It happened to me one fine morning in the spring of 1960, when I entered the Midland Bank in town to open my very first bank account.

I waited my turn at the Enquiries counter, then said, clearly enough: "I'd like to open a bank account, please."

The man behind the counter (this was before glass screens) barely raised his eyes.

"Yes," he said. "What for?"

I cleared my throat and repeated the words.

"But what for?" he asked again, beginning to tap his fingers.

"I just thought it would be a good idea, that's all."

"Yes, yes, I understand that. But *what for?*"

"It's *allowed,* isn't it?"

"Of course it's allowed."

"Not against the law?"

"No, of course not."

"Well then, I'd like to open a bank account so I'll have somewhere to put my money. I've joined the Merchant Navy, you see, and when I'm away at sea I may have some to spare. Up till now I've sort of lived from hand to mouth, as you might say. Well, not *really* hand to mouth - we're not all that poor. My family, I mean - I'm not married. But it's true that my last job didn't pay very well. In fact I'm just out of an apprenticeship, to be honest."

'That's all very interesting, but not very relevant. I just need to know *what for*, that's all. *You* have to tell *me*. I can't read your mind."

"But *Jesus Christ* - I don't know what else to say except that I need a safe place to put my money! Why *else* does anyone open a bloody bank account?"

There was a long pause before the man spoke again.

"Now you look here - coming in a place like this and talking in that tone of voice! I've a good mind to send for the manager and have you thrown out on your ear!... All I'm asking is if you want to open a *deposit* account or a *current* account."

"Oh, I see... Well, perhaps if you could explain the difference."

*

Young men at that time still faced the prospect of two years compulsory service in the armed forces - National Service. This might have been seen as a welcome escape from an already developing rut, but not so many viewed it in that light. Some even feared it, for the basic training was well known for combining incredibly hard but totally pointless physical labour, microscopic attention to smartness of dress, and gross personal insults. The training was designed to cure you of any lingering notions of individuality, and in a word transform you into a *man.*

I knew almost before I knew anything that it wasn't for me. As a rule the call-up age was eighteen, but if you were in an apprenticeship and attending college you could defer entry until twenty-one. Once you had reached that age, however, there weren't many options. You could hope you would fail your medical - because your feet were found to be flat, or your hearing poor. Or you could join one of the exempt occupations, like coal mining or- as in my case -the Merchant Navy. Normally you would have had to stay there for a good many years, but conscription was soon to come to an end, everyone knew. So the decision was easy. As might be expected, though, there was a mad scramble for the Merchant Navy. I only just made it, signing up for my first trip on the very day I received my call-up papers. I had the deep satisfaction of returning them in person.

The line I'd joined had offices down near the Pier Head in Liverpool. I was assigned to the 6000-ton *Pizarro*, currently berthed in a dock almost as far down the Dock Road as Bootle. Before reporting for duty I had to purchase my uniforms - one was for tropical use - with modest braiding appropriate to my rank of Second-Sixth Engineer, plus white overalls and other gear needed for actually working.

Though much relieved at having avoided the dreaded army, I was by no means free from anxiety. Based in Liverpool, I would presumably be sailing with a local crew - a surly and intimidating bunch, in all likelihood. I pictured them as something like the sailors in *Treasure Island* under Long John Silver's command, with black eye patches and all. How could I be expected, as a raw recruit, to muster the necessary physical presence to give orders to such ruffians? And aside from that. what did I know about the workings of a ship's engine room? I scarcely knew how a *canteen boiler* was put together. My deplorable ignorance of "real engineering" would surely now be fully exposed. And would I be *seasick?* The only ship I'd ever sailed on was the ferry across the Mersey to New Brighton.

It was certainly a worrying time, though there were of course more positive things to look forward to, not least the prospect of visiting foreign lands. But all that seemed to lie in the somewhat distant future.

*

Liverpool was still a tremendously busy port. The Dock Road was around three miles long, and there were ships from every nation tied up from one end to the other. I was instructed to report to the Second Engineer of the *Pizarro* - though not for the purpose of doing a day's work, as it transpired. When I had battled my way on my first morning through all the hustle and bustle to his cabin I was simply told that I was one of three junior engineers who would be working a twelve hours on/twenty-four off watch system until we sailed, and should report back at 6pm. The engineer I would be relieving would explain my duties.

I returned in the evening to find the ship outwardly deserted. The swarms of dock workers and maintenance and repair gangs I had seen earlier had melted away, dropping everything where they stood when the signal to finish work had sounded, by the look of it. I could hear a muffled rumbling noise down below, but the only visible sign of life was a thin trail of smoke from the funnel. It looked as if I was going to be in charge of not only the engine room for the night, but, as the only officer on board, of the *whole ship.*

I found the junior I was to relieve in his cabin, already showered and changed and impatient to be off.

"Get your overalls on quick and I'll take you down!" he said. "I'll give you five minutes."

I swiftly changed into a pristine white boiler suit and hurried after him. The din, once inside the engine room, seemed deafening (and the noise was coming from only a single diesel generator, I would later find). We descended five or six flights of metal staircase, which threaded their way through a congestion of vessels and pipes that were a total mystery to me. At last we reached the very lowest level, fifty feet or more below the entrance. Shouting directly into my ear (a practice, I would notice, which readily identified a merchant seaman ashore), he rapidly took a series of dial readings and fuel-oil soundings that I would have to record at intervals, then showed me how to write them up in the log book.

"There'll be plenty of oil for the night," he said finally. "I pumped it earlier."

I was relieved to hear this, though it seemed a minor matter.

"What about everything else?" I bawled, waving a hand about in a vague, futile gesture.

"Don't worry, you'll be able to turn in later. The donkey man will look after the boiler."

"Boiler? Donkey man? Who the hell's the *donkey* man?"

But he was already climbing the steps, leaving me to it.

Well, at least I wasn't going to be alone. Somewhere there lurked a donkey man. Wandering by chance into the boiler room, I found not one man but two, sitting playing cards. As I presumably had authority over them, I thought I'd better introduce myself. My sudden appearance on the scene had so far been ignored.

"I'm the new engineer," I shouted, at close range. My voice was by now beginning to lose strength. "On watch, you know… Which of you is the donkey man?"

One of them raised his eyes.

"I understand you're looking after the boiler. Right?"

The man nodded. You evidently didn't waste words in this place.

"Which boiler is it?"

He indicated with a thumb over his shoulder, then mouthed, "The donkey boiler."

"Well, that makes sense," I laughed. "What's it for, by the way?"

He glanced at his companion.

"Hot water," he seemed to say, before giving his attention back to his cards.

Feeling hardly any wiser, I did a trial run through the log-book data routine, then I climbed the steps back up to the deck. There wasn't a soul about, so I retreated to my cabin, there to reflect on the enormity of being apparently responsible for an entire ship, while having minimal instructions or apparent duties. At ten o'clock I crept down below once more to take my first proper set of readings, my new boiler suit already stained. I found the donkey man sitting alone now, reading a paper.

"OK if I turn in?" I asked him loudly, though doing my best to sound casual, for I could think of no reason why *he* shouldn't be the one to go to bed.

"Fine," he shouted back. Then he handed me his paper. "Read this if you like."

*

Ships of our line sailed to the West Indies and the Pacific coast of South America. The itinerary was attractive, but I hadn't joined for that reason. I'd simply been tipped off that it was one of the easier companies to get into. But I rather liked the way the ships were named after adventurers of old, like *Pizarro*, which added a flavour of romance to our more mundane voyages, as they were officially known.

Some of my first anxieties soon evaporated. For example, although somewhat rough in appearance, the members of the crew turned out to be surprisingly tame, even deferential. Being a Merchant Navy officer was an essentially civilian occupation, but they seemed to think that anyone entitled to wear a uniform - even a green newcomer- must know what he was talking about, or doing, and therefore be treated with respect. Some of the older firemen had spent a lifetime at sea, yet from a technical point of view they were quite ignorant of the workings of the engine-room plant, save for the small part that directly concerned them.

Steam ships by the early 1960s had oil-fired boilers. It relieved the fireman of labour to the point where he had very little to do but clean a fresh set of burners for the next watch.

Otherwise he kept an eye on the boiler water level and pressure, and if these started to go wrong shouted for the engineer, in whose competence he had complete faith.

The other crewman on watch was the somewhat more mysterious - but still under-occupied - *greaser*. He went around with a large oil can, and if anyone was watching, oiled something. Greasers were evidently born with an instinct for what required lubrication. At any rate, I don't recall ever seeing a maintenance schedule of any kind. But random as their duties seemed to be, no piece of machinery ever failed for want of oil to my knowledge. Far from being ruffians, the greasers I encountered were timid creatures, slipping about in the shadows.

That left the day workers. They were not part of the watch as such. Their job was to polish, clean and paint. No preparation was undertaken for the painting. Valve casings, pipe flanges and such were covered time after time, until their features were reduced to a smooth, blended outline, so that the first step in any maintenance task was to expose the nuts and bolts with a chisel. The polishing part of their routine consisted of buffing up odd bits of unpainted copper piping - for purely aesthetic reasons, so far as I could ever make out.

Seasickness turned out not to be a serious problem. You spent days, maybe a week, tied up in port before sailing, so the small movements of the ship prepared you gradually for rougher water. And the manoeuvring stages before the ship reached open sea took several hours as well. It wasn't like boarding a ferry and within minutes finding yourself out in the stormy English Channel.

But my lack of proper engineering experience was another matter. Nor was it easy to find anything out. The tradition was that if you couldn't understand something you went to endless lengths to solve the problem yourself before asking someone, and even then you would be met with sarcasm. But given the deafening noise down below - the whine of the turbines added to the generator racket after we left port - it may well have been the most sensible course, anyway.

The heat was terrible, too. In the tropics the temperature on deck could be way up in the eighties, but you would still feel a blast of warm air as you began your descent. As with the fires of hell, the hottest part of the engine room was also at the deepest level - that is in the boiler room (or stokehold, as it was still referred to), for which the junior engineer on watch was nominally responsible. When it got *really* hot you stood under the blowers, eating salt tablets like sweets.

Then there were the unceasing lurchings of the ship, which were never quite predictable and rendered every task more difficult. Tools or dismantled pieces of equipment left in a place where they could slide about might easily slip through a grating and hit someone beneath - or disappear into the oily, swilling water of the bilges. All the pitching and rolling also meant that you had to use your hands or arms when making your way about, making use of whatever was handy. It didn't help that the original colour-coding of plant and pipework had long since been reduced by the day workers to a single colour, a dirty cream, so that you could no longer recognise a hot pipe or vessel. It led to frequent burns, and with the sleeves of your overalls permanently rolled up your forearms were soon covered in scars. Even up in the saloon you automatically laid anything that might tip over on its side on your dining table.

I imagine that ship's engine rooms are more automated now than fifty years ago. With the *Pizarro,* it was mostly manual operation. When "full away" it was possible to achieve something like a steady-state, but the fluctuating demands for steam during manoeuvring could only be responded to by switching burners on and off and controlling the boiler water feed with a manual valve.

And just up above you on the manoeuvring platform life could be even more hectic. The rule was that the Chief Engineer was supposed to be in control and responding to the telegraphed orders received from the bridge - say: *Full Ahead - Stop - Half Astern - Stop - Half Ahead - Stop - Full Astern* (all perhaps in the space of a minute or so) - but I don't ever recall seeing *our* Chief down below. He would be on the booze up in his cabin, leaving it to the senior engineer on watch - which could be me after I had been made up to Fourth. The loud jangling of the telegraph bell as each instruction was received set your nerves keenly on edge for starters. Then you had to answer the move with your own telegraph (a device you often glimpse in old films}, record it in a register required for insurance purposes, open or close the big valves for Ahead or Astern steam, watch the gland steam pressure, so as not to lose the precious vacuum in the condenser (which would be a *real* disaster, I'd been warned, but fortunately it never happened to me), and in between try to respond to cries of distress from the stokehold. In extreme circumstances you might press the emergency button for assistance, whereupon one of your disturbed colleagues up in the cabins would skilfully insert a piece of cardboard under the little bell hammer to stop the racket.

Yes, the job could be quite tough. Sometimes you wondered if the coal mines, or even the army itself, might have been an easier option. On my first trip we had to get up at a quarter-to-four as well, to be ready for the four-to-eight watch. We had nothing to eat or drink till the watch was nearly over, when the fireman would go up for tea and toast. Breakfast proper didn't happen for us until nine, by which time you'd had to remove your oil-soaked overalls, kick off your filthy, laceless boots, take a shower, and put on a clean white shirt, uniform, and polished black shoes. Eating in the saloon was the only use to which the uniform was ever put.

*

Most of the goods we carried on the *Pizarro* were out of sight down in the holds and a boring mystery, but now and then we had quite unusual items in open view on the decks. In one case our cargo was controversial. At the time of the abortive "Bay of Pigs" invasion of Cuba, we carried highly visible Leyland buses into Havana harbour. Apparently we were shown on the television news back home. The Americans strongly disapproved, but (rather amazingly, as it now seems) the trade was supported publicly by the British Foreign Secretary of the time, Lord Home. I can recall walking the streets of Havana alone, despite the presence there of many armed soldiers. We British were heroes. To show an American dollar in Havana was to risk your life, whereas the sight of a humble British pound (usually despised by comparison) brought forth smiles on the streets, and warmer expressions of gratitude in the dockside bars.

Another time I returned from home shore leave almost at the point of sailing, paying little attention to two rows of large wooden boxes lined up on the aft deck. Later, having reason to visit the aft accommodation, I glanced sideways as I passed the first of the boxes, and was amazed to find myself face-to-face with a *racehorse.* I had been kept in deliberate ignorance. We were carrying a dozen of them down to Buenaventura in Colombia for breeding purposes.

But the most interesting of these deck cargoes was undoubtedly a small travelling circus, on its way from Guayaquil, in Ecuador, down the coast to the Chilean port of Valparaiso. In truth the few circus animals were pretty unimpressive, though they did include a pair of old, rather moth-eaten lions, kept in flimsy cages. Looking up from the pit of the engine room, late at night, I used to wonder what I would do if one of these beasts should suddenly stroll into view up by the entrance.

The Bosun of the *Pizarro* (a kind of foreman in charge of the deck crew), a loner who seemed to walk about in a permanent trance, took it into his head to torment one of them with a stick one evening, while a little group of us were out on deck enjoying the cooler weather. The animal got his revenge, though, for a little later, when the man had his back to the cage, a junior electrician who was fond of practical jokes bent down behind him and tightly gripped his ankle, at the same time doing his best impression of a lion's throaty growl. I only wish I'd had a camera ready.

On the subject of practical jokes, a great favourite which never failed to work - carried out at anchor ports, when the gangplank would be partially lowered to allow bathing in the sea - was to dive in straight after someone, then touch his foot as he surfaced. An accomplice on the ship would then wave to him in alarm, crying, *"SHARRRRKS!"*

*

Doubtless the industry (what little remains of it) has been cleaned up since those days, but on the *Pizarro* you saw a good deal of petty corruption. A lot of it consisted of selling stuff that had been issued in good faith without being strictly essential. There could be quite a business going on when we were tied up in port. A typical example was selling off the new tarpaulin covers that were provided for the hatches each trip. Everybody knew the originals, dating back to when the ship was built, were still in place - and still in reasonable condition. Another commodity popular with eager port contacts was paint, supplies of which were always far too generous. But even food and drink were sold. I once saw cases of English tinned food being quietly carried ashore, to be replaced by Peruvian merchandise of doubtful quality. That was on our outward journey. Heading home, our Chief Steward let go our entire stock of canned lager, so that re-crossing the Atlantic we were left with only Guinness to sustain us, for which some of us had quickly to acquire a taste.

But I was most entertained by a particularly outrageous piece of salesmanship involving again our unfriendly Bosun. After many requests, the *Pizarro* had finally been provided with a swimming pool - a modest affair, to be sure, made from wood and canvas, which could be drained and collapsed in fifteen minutes, but which when erected offered some relief from the tropical heat, even if a couple of languid breast strokes carried you easily over its full length. The Bosun was responsible for the pool but persuading him to erect and fill it was a battle. He had an iron rule he'd invented himself that it couldn't be put up until we had passed through the Panama Canal, and had to be taken down again before we reached Valparaiso. He was much nagged, of course, and finally responded to this harassment in characteristic fashion. Late one night - in Callao or somewhere, when everyone was ashore in the bars - he *sold* it. No one witnessed the transaction - the official explanation was that it had been stolen. And given his normal trance-like state it was impossible to be completely certain that he was drunker than usual afterwards. But nobody had any real doubt.

We engineers remained on the fringes of this behaviour, though we weren't above selling our free-issue bottle of spirits to the locals who came swarming aboard in certain ports, if strapped for cash. Perfume, however, was a vastly more prized commodity than whisky or rum. Evidently their girlfriends and others couldn't get enough of it - especially Yardley. One or two of the more mature officers would stock up with it before sailing.

From time to time there were attempts to suppress this business, trifling as it was, but the crackdowns were never very effective tor the simple reason that the corruption extended to the highest levels on both sides. Still, both sides had to be careful. One evening, in Valparaiso, when everyone but the poor sods down below had gone ashore, I had remained in my cabin, to take advantage of the comparative peace to write a letter. Suddenly I heard a patter of feet in the corridor, followed by a tapping at my door. Before I could leave my chair the door burst open and a fat little man in uniform, with medals and braid to equal an admiral, leapt in, hugging a stupendous collection of bottles and boxes and packets of perfume, talc, soap and other toiletries, with the brand name Yardley much in evidence. On his hip he carried a gun. He closed the door quietly with his bottom, and stood with his back to it, panting for breath.

"So sorry," he said at last, noticing me. That seemed to exhaust his English. With occasional little smiles and knowing looks in my direction, he proceeded carefully to hide every item about his person. His uniform seemed to have cleverly designed inside pockets, so that when he had finished he presented a smooth outline, with no suspicious bulges. He patted himself here and there, then, touching his cap, vanished just as quickly as he had made his entrance. I hadn't said a word.

*

When it came to smuggling goods back into the UK, we were generally content with extra cartons of cigarettes and bottles of whiskey. Even so, the customs men hunted down these things with the same patience and cunning they would nowadays apply to searching for heroin or cocaine. Consequently it was hardly worth the bother, especially if, like me, you neither smoked, nor drank spirits, yourself. My heart wasn't in it, but this didn't stop me having a number of near scrapes, and one memorable instance of being caught red-handed.

Having taken home my normal allowance on the day we reached port, I returned next morning, imagining the customs officials would have moved on, to retrieve a further two-hundred cigarettes that I had stashed away in individual packets by unscrewing the panelling of my day-bed. These were strewn about my cabin, and I had only just replaced all the screws, when there was a sudden rapping on the door. I opened it an inch, and was shocked to see two uniformed men outside, who pushed their way in without waiting to be invited. I had managed to conceal the screwdriver, but the scene looked highly suspicious, to put it mildly.

Quick thinking was called for, though the best I could do to answer their questions was to brazenly point out that the cigarettes in fact added up precisely to my permitted quota. They countered this, however, with a warning that a quick phone call was all that would be needed to arrange a search at my home address to check if any more cigarettes happened to be lying around there. It would only take twenty minutes. I well knew that my legitimate carton of two-hundred would be in full view on top of the sideboard, where I had casually tossed it, and was close to confessing - when their eyes lighted on my watch, lying on my desk. It was a working day, and I had taken it off before putting in an appearance in the engine room, which was normal procedure. We had a clock down there.

The cigarettes were instantly forgotten. Here was a find they could *really* get their teeth into.

In fact I had bought the watch on a previous trip and paid full duty. I told them as much, but a form was produced for me to sign. At the top, in bold letters, it explained that the maximum fine for false information was £600. Did I wish to reconsider?

At that point there was another knock on the door, and the Second Engineer's head appeared. I had forgotten that I had to show a party of sea cadets around the engine room. With a show of reluctance, the men said they would allow me to attend to the cadets (likely to be an ordeal in itself) while they went down to check the manifest for the previous voyage at Customs House. I returned to my cabin an hour later to find one of the men standing outside my door, shaking his head.

"I can't believe it," I said, still recovering from the cadets.

"Well, we've been to have a look, and it's there in black and white." He produced the worrying form once more. "Now, if you'll sign this it will save us all a lot of trouble, believe me."

I thought for a moment.

"But don't you mean the watch is *not* there on the manifest in black and white?"

"Yes, of course. It's *missing* in black and white. I mean… "

"Look, if you'll give me till tomorrow morning, I'm *sure* I'll be able to find the duty receipt at home."

He peered closely at his watch. as if checking tomorrow morning's time. "Make it eleven sharp," he said, with a final show of authority.

In truth, I hadn't the smallest confidence that I'd be able to find the vital bit of paper. I had been playing for time. But when I looked, there it was, at the top of the very first drawer I opened.

Next morning, at eleven sharp, I was more than ready for the man.

But - surprise surprise! - he failed to show up.

4
CHILTERN ENGINERRING

I left the Merchant Navy abruptly, after two years. National Service had, as predicted, now come to an end, and I'd had thoughts of getting out in any case. But I left under a cloud.

A day or two before we were due to sail on what would be my last trip I had scalded my right foot badly. I'd been a little careless, but it *was* an accident. At least I could claim as much. This was in the days before modern Health-and-Safety rules. You were supposed to watch what you were doing, and I hadn't. Not closely enough, anyway, although I rather kept that to myself.

Well, if I didn't sail with the *Pizarro* there would be a significant delay while a replacement was found. That would be costly. So I agreed to sail provided I could take time off on the Atlantic crossing, the quietest part of any voyage. This was accepted.

I spent several days in my bunk, but was beginning to hobble about by the time we reached the Bahamas, though still in a lot of pain. Walking wasn't *too* bad, but if I stopped I had to rest my foot in a raised position, or the throbbing would be unbearable. So I was in no fit state to work. In the meantime others were having to stand in for me. What I didn't know was that the impression was beginning to spread that I was malingering. Only when we had manoeuvred our way through the Panama Canal - which meant longer shifts - was I seriously able to resume light duties.

It was then, as we were reaching the more interesting stops down the coast, that a decision was made that I was to do extra time on board ship while in port to compensate for my earlier time off, leaving the others free to spend more time in the bars. It came out of the blue - just as I was getting into my stride once more - and I naturally made a fuss. There was a great *row* in fact, but no compromise. I was told it would mean that my foot would have even *more* time to heal itself, and I surely wasn't going to say no to that. Life on the *Pizarro* became very bitter for me.

Even so, back in Liverpool, I wasn't expecting to be summoned into the Superintendent Engineer's office for a quiet chat. He said he'd heard about my "differences" with the other engineers on the *Pizarro,* and had decided it would be best for all concerned if I were moved immediately to another vessel. In fact the necessary arrangements had already been made.

I found myself telling him, without forethought, that his plans would need further amendment, since I had no wish to stay on the *Pizarro,* or to move to another ship, or to stay with his company, or indeed to continue with a career in the Merchant Navy *at all.* Thus it was that I found myself five minutes later standing outside in the street, on a wet November day in 1961, without a job.

It *seemed* very sudden, but my subconscious mind had definitely been at work for some time. I had never intended to make the Merchant Navy my life. It was very much a young man's game. You encountered hardly anyone over thirty, and those who *did* make it a career became rather strange - mentally somewhat dull and distant - or so it seemed to me. Our Bosun, in his fifties at a guess, was an extreme case. Maybe the constant movements of the ship were a factor, along with living in what amounted to a closed community, or being separated from wives and families for months on end, visiting foreign lands without ever getting to know very much about them, relieving the hours of boredom with drink, being drawn into superficially enviable but in truth worthless relationships with the girls in the bars, having no real friends whether at home or away - all of these things could have contributed to a gradual breakdown of personality for the few who became trapped in the life.

Yes, it was time to leave the sea - as a matter of urgency!

*

But what next? Well, thanks to my bank account I had saved quite a bit of money, so I wasn't in a desperate position. I took a few weeks holiday, then I wrote to my old firm, Modern Age, to see if they'd consider taking me back. I was informed that they felt no obligation to do so, and had no vacancy at present.

Oh dear. I hadn't exactly been counting on it, but then nor had I expected to be rebuffed in a couple of lines. It began to dawn on me that I was going to have to re-establish myself as a draughtsman. A job couldn't be taken for granted. There was a lot of unemployment at that time, too. The economy was having to try to absorb the young men who would have been in the forces for two years. Nor could I claim to be fully qualified. Apart from my inadequate apprenticeship, I had not passed my Higher National, normally regarded as the minimum qualification for admittance to a drawing office.

I looked in the papers, and was alarmed to see very few positions for draughtsmen advertised. Next, I tried the Labour Exchange (as such places were then called). They had nothing except a few clerical jobs, and I would need 0' levels for those.

Christmas and New Year passed. I began to be depressed - nor was I helped by a newspaper article I read which claimed that, after doctors, draughtsmen were more prone than others to suicide - something to do with the meticulous nature of the work. I wondered what the statistics were for draughtsmen who couldn't *find* a job.

On leaving the sea, I had vaguely thought it might be a moment to try for a career change. I'd always wanted to be an artist, or writer, and I had money in the bank, as I've said, to keep me going. But that too was hopeless. Even more hopeless, in fact. It wasn't even possible to get into a *conversation* with anyone on the subject. Once a draughtsman *always* a draughtsman was very much the rule. Never mind that there were no actual jobs to be *had* for draughtsmen. This wasn't the bleakest moment in my working life (as will be seen), though it came close.

But I kept diligently looking in the papers each evening - what else could I do? - and at last, carelessly turning its pages, I came across a tiny advertisement in the *Manchester Evening News,* placed there at the least possible cost. "Draughtsman wanted. Apply Chiltern Engineering" was all it said. Plus a phone number. There wasn't even an address.

I phoned nervously from a call box, asking where they were. They said they would write, giving directions and offering me an interview. No questions were put to me. Their letter when it came was short, informing me that the wage would be ten pounds a week, *if* I was suitable. Latterly, in the Merchant Navy, my salary had approached a hundred pounds a month (and with bed and board taken care of). But to hell with all that, I thought - I *needed* this job!

I learned from the address that I would be facing a ten mile journey each day, and using public transport would have been difficult, but luckily I had access to our family car, an old Morris Minor. My father, at Modern Age still, worked much closer to home and - coming to my rescue again - said he'd go back to using his bike. It hadn't really occurred to me how much anxiety I was causing my parents.

Chiltern's letter-head included a simplified view of what I assumed was their factory. It looked to be quite impressive - probably a converted mill of some sort. As I neared the neighbouring town I scanned the skyline. There were several possibilities, but their location didn't fit the directions I'd been sent. Finally, I was led to a short cobbled street in a slum area. One entire side of the premises was a high, windowless wall, in old brick, badly in need of pointing. Down at the far end I could see a single green door, alongside double gates, and by the door I found a dull brass nameplate that told me I had reached my destination. This was the actual frontage that the designer of the letter-head had taken such liberties with.

The receptionist was more attractive. In what sounded surprisingly like a southern accent, she told me to wait - there was no chair she could offer - while she contacted the man I was to see, a Mr Jennings (though for some reason the letter I'd received had been signed by somebody else). After a wait - with secret glances at the girl - I was at last led up a dimly-lit staircase to a brighter corridor, and his office.

Mr Jennings (Alec, I soon learned) had a worried look and was thin to the point of emaciation. In consequence, he appeared taller than he actually was. He had a small moustache, and a mass of brown hair that had a tendency to fall into his eyes.

"So you found us, then?" he began. with a nervous chuckle. "I was getting a bit anxious - thought you weren't going to bother... You'll have to excuse the state of this place. We've been advertising for a cleaner for three months... Here, have a seat - I won't take your coat. Don't lean too far back on these chairs. I got them cheap from a second-hand furniture store down the road. Ten bob apiece... Excuse the hair. I haven't been able to get to the barber's for weeks... I bet they didn't warn you what to expect in the letter."

"Well, no..."

"They tore mine up. It was too honest."

"Really?... Who are *they,* by the way?"

"Jarvis and Lord. The Works Manager and Managing Director. You won't be meeting *them* today."

"Why's that?"

"I don't intend *introducing* you. They'd scare you away."

"I see... But will they let *you* make the decision?"

"Oh yes - provided I don't offer you more money. Did they tell you the wage?"

"Ten pounds, yes."

"I thought as much. And strictly no negotiation... So I suppose you won't be staying?"

"I don't see why not. I'm satisfied with ten pounds."

"Satisfied?"

"Well, yes. I've been in the Merchant Navy, you see. Instead of the army, you know. And to be honest, I've been having trouble getting back into draughting. I'd work for *five* pounds for starters. For *free,* even."

"You must be daft!"

'Very likely."

Alec Jennings seemed hardly to believe that I was on the level, but slowly the interview took on a more formal tone. It emerged that I would be concerned with the shop-fitting side of Chiltern's business - designing shelving and counter units, laying out shop conversions to self-service (at that time in full swing), and preparing estimates. This struck me as pretty interesting stuff - compared, say, with my work at Modern Age - though I could envisage that the job might not improve my marketability in the real engineering game.

"When can you start?"

"I was thinking maybe next Monday."

He seemed crestfallen at this.

"I could leave it longer, if you like."

"Longer?... To tell you the truth, I was hoping you might agree to stay *today.* Things are pretty desperate here, and those two don't help."

"Jarvis and Lord?"

"Yes - it's harassment at every turn. But they leave me to face the music with the customers."

"I see. Well, I hope I can be useful. But I'd prefer to leave it at least until tomorrow, all the same."

We shook hands on that, then I made my way back down to the receptionist, who had lingered in my mind as a bit of an anomaly in this distinctly peculiar establishment.

*

During the interview I had wondered where precisely I would be working. Alec Jennings' office contained a drawing board and a desk, but that left scarcely enough room to swing a cat round. I hadn't enquired because I guessed he might be afraid of running into his hated superiors if we went to look. I thought it was also the likely reason why I hadn't been taken to see the shop floor. But these things had simply slipped his mind - or so he indicated next morning - because of the nature of the interview.

Well, it turned out that the working conditions for me would not be as disagreeable as I might have feared, tor a larger, pretty conventional drawing office was almost ready for occupation. The plan was eventually to recruit a third draughtsman, and maybe even more, so as to begin to assemble a "design team". Alec Jennings himself, though, would have to stay in his present cramped office, where he was conveniently on hand as a punchbag for Jarvis and Lord.

But there was a special surprise awaiting me in this new office. At first I could hardly believe it - something I'd only *dreamed* of. The board I was to work on had a *draughting machine* attached - the device that Jim McNulty had turned his back on with such contempt. It was a pretty rudimentary model, to be sure, that Alec had picked at up cheaply, like the chairs - controlled by a spring rather than the usual balance weight, so that you nearly sprained your wrist if you moved the draughting head to the extremities of the drawing surface. In fact he had planned to fit it to his own board, despite the limited space. But seeing my pleasure at the prospect of using it, he agreed to leave it where it was and shop around for another.

"You don't know how *rare* these things are," I told him. "Even the very *biggest* companies often don't have them, I've heard."

'Then I can only think they're not under the same kind of pressure to turn out the drawings as *we* are."

Chiltern's more established business, I learned, was manufacturing paraffin heaters and carpet-sweepers, which reached the public via a big mail-order firm. Alec Jennings, who had little previous drawing-board experience (he was a sheet-metal worker by trade), had somehow been brought in a few years previously to help in an effort to diversify, the worry being that the traditional products might have little mileage left in them. Alec's chief creation to date was a flexible range of shelving, which was selling well, though this new line of business was also bringing headaches. Shop conversions needed to go like clockwork, so as to avoid excessive business disruption, but they rarely did. There was always *some* item that didn't fit, which led to angry complaints and demands to speak to the Manager - or even the Managing *Director.* The result was that Alec's tormentors often hankered after the simplicity of the older, traditional products, which required no sales, distribution or installation effort. The shop-fittings customers, I gathered, had begun to refer sarcastically to the company as "Chiltern *Enginerring*".

That was how things stood when I began to clock-in at Chiltern's. Alec Jennings, nearing thirty, was harassed by impossible problems, but couldn't withdraw because, with no technical qualifications whatever, he would probably have a much harder time than I would finding other draughting work. He had to make a success of the shop-fittings business. He also had plans for extending the range of equipment to include more sophisticated items, like refrigerated units. But with the constant carping of the management and the great difficulty in recruiting competent staff, these plans were lost to view, and he was in danger of going under.

*

Settled soon in the new drawing office, I half expected Jarvis and Lord to burst in at any moment like a sort of demented music-hall act. But for some time I didn't knowingly encounter either of them. Then one day a heavy, gasping individual with nicotine-stained wavy grey hair and thick glasses with black frames stopped by to introduce himself - in a pleasant enough manner. This was Jarvis. Lord, I discovered, was seldom on the premises. Apparently the group had a few other small factories dotted about, and he spent his time shuttling between them. I did glimpse him now and then - a shifty-looking, smartly-dressed man with thinning black hair scraped hard against his skull - but no words were exchanged, and he seemed to have no curiosity about me at all.

The more recent and as yet straightforward enquiries were steered in my direction. Alec continued to grapple with the accumulated mess, while attempting to placate and keep at bay angry customers. Jarvis in particular presumably remained on his back, but, a safe distance away,

I witnessed none of their disputes. Alec had to approve my schemes and estimates, thus lining himself up for any of the flak that might arise from my mistakes. In sort, I was in a protected position. And soon I was trusted to go out on site visits alone. This kind of release was a new and even heady experience for me, remembering my total imprisonment at Modern Age. And I could also claim (very meagre) *travelling expenses.*

So things seemed to be going pretty well. A young apprentice was taken on, relieving me of a number of routine tasks. Then Jarvis stumbled into the office again, as if by accident, but stayed long enough to tell me between gasping breaths (he was a heavy smoker) that my work seemed up to scratch and I could expect to see an extra couple of pounds in my pay packet.

Confidence in the shop-fitting side of the business improved, until at last the heat seemed to be off. Alec Jennings, now shorn and neat, was free to give more attention to his pet scheme - a new line of refrigerated cabinets. The only cloud in those early months was a conflict in our basic purposes.

I was intent on re-establishing myself as a draughtsman, and didn't much care about the viability of the company or anything like that. But Alec, closer to the customers, was more switched on to what might now be called the "business needs". He may even have had some thought about advancing in the firm, now that his relations with his bosses were a little better. For him, a drawing needed only to convey basic information, whereas for me - a disciple of Jim McNulty- it was an end in itself. I was all for producing what he was apt to dismiss as "pretty pictures" - thinking of the future, and wanting to have work in my portfolio (not that I had such a thing for real) to impress a less harassed employer. But otherwise we got along well enough.

*

"Is't gain' t'ask yon lass aht, or what?" our new apprentice asked me one day. This was the local dialect - more recognisable English was barely spoken in the small, isolated town I was working in. Alec Jennings and I had both grown up not too far away in miles, but at quite a distance linguistically, though our accents were far from posh.

Our apprentice was a frizzy-haired though good-looking teenager called Donald, who had quickly become something a disciple of mine. A *what?* Well, I was by now a *Guardian* reader·- fancying myself as an intellectual - and he was ready to soak up my opinions on the social and political issues of the day. But he was ahead of me in two respects. The Beatles were beginning to make an impression, and he insisted that they were going to be very big indeed. I had to beg to differ. And despite barely needing to shave, he was a good deal more successful with the girls than I was.

Not that I was any longer a total loss. The dockside bars of South America had pretty much cured me of my adolescent blushing, though I was still surprisingly green - and idealistic. Not a good combination. I had yet to find a steady girlfriend. The kind of girl I believed I was really looking for was one I could talk to on the same intellectual level - while being quite unaware that in more fundamental ways I was a complete ignoramus. What's more, I even imagined that the way to a girl's heart might be through the many important books I'd read. So it was in this state of mind that I had said to young Donald that I felt our receptionist, with her refined southern accent, might be the type to appreciate this kind of approach. Hence his question. I had been dragging my feet far too long.

The girl's name was Sheila - a name that meant more to me than most, for the first two girls I had had secret crushes on in my life had both been Sheilas. That was back at primary school in the I 940s. After a little spadework, I discovered that this Sheila lived on my way to work - not on my direct route, but only a minor detour was needed - and used the bus. All I had to do was to contrive to be just ahead of the bus she would be catching, and I could offer her a lift. It was harder to do than you might think, but before long I had her sitting next to me in the passenger seat of the old Morris Minor most mornings. Smart work!

I learned that she was around twenty, from a broken home, and had moved north for an indefinite period to live with an aunt. Almost a damsel in distress! And from her conversation, I easily convinced myself that she was in need of more stimulating chat than she'd enjoyed in the north so far. Naturally, I felt perfectly qualified to fill this role. And for a while she *did* seem eager to listen to my newly-acquired radical notions. Soon - as in a Woody Allen fantasy - I even had her reading one or two of my favourite books. This actually went on for a couple of months. I also took her out for a drink now and again. Then one day she told me she had a boyfriend still, back in her home town, and was considering heading south once more to move into a flat with him. What did I think of the idea?

After that I took less trouble to manoeuvre myself into a position just ahead other bus. Then I reverted to my old route. And only a few weeks later - like Gillian Wade back at Modern Age - this latest Sheila abruptly left Chiltern's without a goodbye. Yet another "romance" had fizzled out.

Meanwhile, Donald's more direct love life was forging ahead!

*

Under the strain of this non-affair my work had been suffering. Sheila's leaving in fact marked the end of my honeymoon period at Chiltern's. Never keen on the side of the job that required careful thought and planning, I was now more than ever inclined to indulge my artistic gifts, such as they were. This did not go unnoticed.

"Well, are you going to frame it?" Alec Jennings enquired one day, as I worked on an elaborately shaded perspective view of a proposed refrigerated cabinet he had designed.

"I might at that," I replied.

This visibly irritated him.

"Look, I *told* you that they only asked for something simple. Just an *impression*. Why *this?*"

"I thought it would be a good illustration we could show to other customers. To help sales, you know."

"But we can't *afford* to work like that. We haven't the resources. If a customer asks for something specific we give him what he wants. No more, no less."

"But is the customer always right?" I asked lazily.

"Damned right he is! And while you're fiddling about with this the enquiries are piling up. You're lucky- you haven't *got* a phone. Nor a bloody Works Manager breathing down your neck. So get your *finger* out!"

"OK," I said. "I'll soon have it finished now. A copy will be ready for you first thing tomorrow morning, without fail."

I knew that things were going wrong but felt powerless, or simply not motivated enough, to head off the coming trouble. And soon complaints of errors in my work began to arrive from the sites I was handling. Alec was first in the firing line, however, so I wasn't yet feeling the flak direct. He would enter my office in a rage, but then would draw back from the kind of ultimatum that was becoming justified. I felt more sorry for him than I did for myself. One day, though, he informed me that he had felt compelled to report on my shortcomings to Jarvis, who had ordered him to join Donald and me in the drawing office, so as to be able to keep a closer eye on my work.

This move at last had the effect of making me understand that I was in serious trouble, and to resolve to perform more competently in future.

*

Only after Alec Jennings had moved in did I fully appreciate the pressure he was under. His telephone had moved office with him, and Jarvis was frequently on it, starting at eight-thirty each morning. Few things are more unsettling than that. In any job you need time to review the work situation before you're ready to face new challenges. My guess was that the man was preparing his probing questions the previous day, but then holding them back so as to catch Alec off balance. The first conversation could last for twenty minutes, and then Jarvis might ring again before Alec had had time to do anything about the previous call. The Works Manager's stamina on the phone was hard to imagine, but very real.

And then there were the customers. One of the moral defects of the market system must surely be what it does to human beings in the buyer-seller relationship. Even the most unlikely person in any business will swell with indignation if, as the customer, he feels his demands are not being properly and promptly attended to. The abuse that Chiltern's customers were ready to shout into the phone, even if their complaint was trivial, took your breath away. Even so, although Alec had not yet put up a sign proclaiming that the customer was always right, that was the essence of his attitude…

After he had endured a particularly humiliating tirade one day, I asked.him:

"How much are they paying you for taking that kind of crap?"

"You cheeky bugger!" He glanced up the office at Donald.

"Come off it," I said quietly *"You* know what I earn."

"Yes, but I am your boss."

"Even so, what do they *pay?"*

"Well… seventeen pounds at present."

"Jesus!" I said. "But that's only five more pounds than *I'm* paid, and you've got a wife and kids to support."

"I know. I started on *eight*… But I thought you weren't interested in money."

"I'm not - desperately. But I'd have to be paid a lot more than that to stand in *your* shoes… Why not ask them for a rise? And at least drop the pretence of respecting the customer when you don't have to."

Alec was extremely restless after that. Then, late in the afternoon, he suddenly shot out of the office without saying a word, but slamming the door as he went.

Ten minutes later he came slowly back, pale and shaken. "Anything doing?" I asked.

He shook his head.

The next thing to happen was that another of my installations went slightly wrong. By now I was working well once more, and the problem this time amounted only to bad luck - a single faulty dimension had had the effect of causing a unit to interfere with the opening of a storeroom door. Substituting a shorter unit would be easy enough, and disruption in the meantime not serious, but Jarvis - and Lord also, who happened to be in town - hit the roof when they heard about it. Alec returned from a dressing down with the strict command that he must personally check every single aspect of my work in future. He was the one who had hired me. Meanwhile we could both forget about wage rises indefinitely.

Since the new instructions could not conceivably be carried out, Alec Jennings reacted with uncharacteristic humour. He'd picked up somewhere a piece of transparent plastic material, tinted a deep pink.

This he brought around to my board. Gazing through it at my current piece of work, he pronounced himself satisfied that it could not possibly contain a single error. I then pointed to another drawing, lying on my table, and asked if he would mind looking over that.

"Certainly sir," he said, in a brisk, salesman-like manner. First holding the drawing vertically in front of his face, he then lowered it slowly until his eyes were above the top edge.

5
BERTRAND RUSSELL AND THE BIGOTS

Alec Jennings had joined me on the mildly subversive side of Chiltern's organisation. I was beginning to think of escape. He felt that moving on would be more difficult for him, but he no longer had a dosed mind. For some months we drifted on like that - both fed up - and then the climax came rather suddenly.

One day, in what must have been early 1964, our solitary salesman, Barry Shaw, hinted that something might be afoot and I should watch out. He then told me of a little firm he knew, makers of refrigerated equipment. who were looking for draughtsmen, sixteen pounds a week. I immediately wrote to them, and after an interview was offered a job. Next morning, in work, I composed a triumphant resignation letter and asked Alec to hand it to Jarvis. Rarely in life do you get the chance to speak the truth to your employers, sol wasn't going to miss it.

I said that on the whole I'd done a good job - badly needed in the early days - but because of a few minor slips I had been treated like a child. It was hard for draughtsmen to conceal their mistakes - they even had to list them in the modifications columns on their drawings - whereas shop-floor tradesmen could usually throw theirs in the bin and start again. Other workers, too, had plenty of scope for concealing their errors - even managers. But then to command that a draughtsman must never make another one, and try to give a colleague with more than enough on his plate already responsibility for making it stick - well, that was plain silly. It would only have the effect of demotivating both, and that made future mistakes more likely than ever. I concluded by saying that I'd found a better position with another company, whose management appeared to be a good deal more enlightened.

Alec returned after ten minutes, looking strangely bewildered. He tossed the screwed-up letter in my direction.

"He say it doesn't apply," he explained. "A redundancy letter is on its way to you in the post."

"What?"

"It seems they're taking on a new man."

"Is that so? Well, you might have told me!"

"It was new to me, too."

"Surely not."

Alec nodded. "And they won't tell me anything about him, either."

"But that's ridiculous!"

Already fired up at having my resignation letter - of which I had been rather proud - so casually dismissed, I was further incensed by this outrageous piece of deceit. I smoothed out the crumpled paper and marched straight back to Jarvis's office with it. But I was surprised when I burst in to find that he was not alone. Lord was in town again.

They both looked up when I entered, then turned their backs on me... But I had lost a little of my fire. I became interested in what they were examining on the desk, and saw that it was a typed letter. Was it addressed to the new man, setting out terms and conditions? I guessed that it might be, and on an impulse snatched it from under their noses.

As I sprinted back to the drawing office I was able to check that I was right. I also saw the phrase "to take charge", and the weekly wage that was being offered - "twenty pounds".

Alec Jennings read the letter quickly through when I handed it to him. He was to be replaced as head of the drawing office - that was as much as he needed to know. He reached for his coat.

"I'm off," he said. "Coming?"

I expected it would be just a brief walk-out, but over coffee in the town we decided to make it permanent. We went back next day only to terminate our employment officially and collect our belongings. That was the last either of us ever saw of Chiltern Engineering. Alec Jennings had quietly had his eye on a new job as well, it turned out, and he went on to prosper in it. I was less fortunate.

*

Looking back, mine must have been about the least planned career in drawing-office history. Choice never played much of a part, because I never had much option but to follow the path Fate seemed to have laid out for me. This latest move, to Custom Refrigeration, in a grim suburb of Manchester, would otherwise have to be seen as a crazy one.

As to my claim in my resignation that the management of the new firm were more enlightened, that was pure moonshine. At the interview stage I hadn't liked the look of the people in charge - nor of the place itself. The small works was somehow embedded in a grimy confluence of apparently disused Victorian railway viaducts, with no light anywhere. And the drawing office itself - a long, narrow rectangle - was absolutely devoid of windows to the outside world. One end of it was in fact glazed, but the partition only separated us from the Manager's office. The glass was of the opaque kind, but for a single clear pane in the middle. Every part of the office was commanded by that spy-window. It reminded me of the telescreens in *Nineteen Eighty-Four.*

Not the least crazy aspect of this new job was the daily journey it entailed. There wasn't much point in using the car, since I would have had to cross central Manchester in the rush hour - and rush hours then were worse than they are today. So that left the train - for the main part of the journey, that is. But first I had a two-mile bus ride into town, plus a longish walk to the station. Then, at the Manchester end (this was the old Central Station - now the G-Mex Centre), I actually kept an old bike in the left-luggage office. I wheeled it through the crush of commuters, out onto the city streets, to complete the journey with a hazardous two- mile cycle ride through the busy streets.

Although closer in time, my six months at Custom Refrigeration are harder to call to mind than any other period of my working life. It could be old age, but a more likely explanation is that I have done my best over the years to suppress my recollections of that sorry time.

I do recall that the work itself was peculiar, and very laborious. At Chiltern's, I had grown used to the pleasant convenience of a draughting machine. In this new office, no one would have heard of such a device. We worked not on tilted, separate drawing boards, but on a continuous, horizontal "laying-out" table. Traditional tee-squares and set-squares were used, but your tee-square had to be located against the near-side edge of the table, so that the blade ran perpendicularly away from you. When you put your triangular set-square into position, from where you stood you were faced with having to draw along its bottom edge. The contortions necessary to put lines on paper were something like those of a snooker player who stretches, with one leg up on the table, for an awkward shot, instead of using the rest.

And we weren't producing proper drawings at all. We used thick cartridge paper, the result then being taken to the Joiner's Shop, or some other department, to be used as a kind of template. There was certainly no need for any artistic input. At Chiltern's, I had quietly been honing my drawing skills - with Jim McNulty's rare technique as ever my goal. Now all that was suspended. Everything seemed to have to be executed in a severely practical manner, with no personality flourishes of any kind.

The company, as its name implied, had few standard products. The most memorable was a macabre range of mortuary units, sized and listed in the sales catalogue according to body capacity. But the main work of the office was with freezer chests and refrigerated cabinets for self-service shops and the few supermarkets that then existed. Every job was slightly different and required a new set of "drawings", regardless of how closely it resembled something that had gone before, which was extraordinarily tedious, of course.

*

Barry Shaw, back at Chiltern's, had said they were recruiting draughtsmen, but I was certainly the only newcomer. My new colleagues were all also local men, so far as I could tell. Certainly I was the only one arriving on a bike after a twenty-mile journey.

Anything I said or did could therefore be attributed to my mysterious place of origin. I was regarded as an outsider well before it was established that that was in fact a fair description of my personality. Drawing offices are normally quiet places, but this one had more of the atmosphere of a workshop, in as much as mock abuse was flung about all day long. The glazed partition had its spy-window, but it appeared to be impervious to sound. Now in *my* mid-twenties, I was far from tongue-tied and could trade insults with anybody. But returning the blows could be hard against a well co-ordinated team effort.

I was also on my own in my attitude to the working methods I have described. I couldn't believe the procedure was sensible, and yet no one had the slightest sympathy with my feelings of irritation. They accepted it all as the way life was. You did the work that was expected of you, in the prescribed manner, or you went to work elsewhere. Little point in wasting time trying to think of ways to *improve* how things were done. As to the aesthetics of engineering draughtsmanship, it took me a while to grasp (if I ever did) that the very plainest style possible was what was required. Along the way my instinctively more artistic approach attracted a good deal of derisive comment, naturally enough.

But it was in the realm of more general attitudes and ideas that I was most isolated. To a man, the people at Custom Refrigeration were hangers, floggers, racists, war-enthusiasts, women-abusers, and general all-round bigots. At least that was the clear impression that soon formed in my mind. I realise now that back in those days - as a *Guardian* reader, and lately a big fan of the books of the rebel philosopher Bertrand Russell- I was very quick to rise to the defence of what I saw as civilised opinions. Indeed, I felt far more strongly about such things than

I did about anything that concerned me directly. So there was really no stopping me. And it isn't hard to see now that there was probably quite a bit of exaggeration and baiting going on that I simply didn't notice. Certainly these people were capable of surprising me, as will be seen.

*

I've complained about the train journey I had each day, but it gave me a valuable opportunity to read. An academic failure, I had found myself drawn for the first time to bookshops, there being several good ones in Manchester. I wasn't involved so much in a belated attempt to acquire a little education at last - more a search for kindred spirits, I think. I had also joined CND, and my hero Bertrand Russell had been in the news a good deal in connection with the campaign against nuclear weapons. At the personal level he was as remote from me as could possibly be, for he had been born, in a distant age, into the privileged life of an ancient aristocrat family, and had become one of the greatest scholars in the long and distinguished history of Trinity College, Cambridge. But I didn't give a damn about any of that. What mattered to me, along with the nuclear-weapons issue, was that he was the supreme intellectual rebel of his age, as Voltaire had been a century or more before him. On the train each morning I was devouring the Unwin paperbacks of his more popular and accessible works, then readily available in the shops.

Well, one day I read with excitement in the *Guardian* that Russell, then nearly ninety-two, was to address a meeting in Manchester's Free Trade Hall. I ate in town on the appointed evening, and at seven-thirty joined the fairly large gathering of curious or interested people entering the hall, convinced that to see and hear the man in the flesh was going to be a wonderfully thrilling experience.

He walked onto the stage in sprightly enough fashion, it's true, but when his turn came to speak he had the greatest difficulty delivering his speech. His voice was by now very weak and broken, and he seemed also to be handicapped by a cold. The performance contrasted sharply with his writings, which even at that late stage in his life and career were still remarkably fresh and vigorous. There was no avoiding the fact that he was quite a let down, although I managed to come away believing that, even so, there had been something strangely awe-inspiring about his speech - like being addressed, through an imperfect medium, by an enlightened being from another planet.

Next morning, in work, I was foolish enough to try to say something of this to the decidedly *un*kindred spirits with whom I shared an office.

"Wasn't he that funny old bugger who used to sit down in Trafalgar Square?" said one bigot.

"Ban the bomb!" put in another.

"A bloody headcase, if you ask me!" added a third.

"So *that's* how you spend your evening!" laughed a fourth.

"Well, I'm surprised any of you has even heard of the man," I replied, "seeing that you all take such pride in being so bloody *pig-ignorant.*"

"At least we weren't born without brains altogether, like you people from that God-forsaken suburb of Liverpool," countered the first bigot.

"I live a safe distance from both Liverpool and Manchester," I told them. "Consequently we're mercifully in no danger of inheriting any of the congenital idiocy that's rife in any big city."

This was nonsense, in as much as it's the people in isolated places who are most likely to be affected in that way. But it earned me a brief silence, so I went on to say, "If it wasn't for men like Russell, taking a stand against nuclear weapons, the politicians and the generals would have blown us all to smithereens by now."

"But we've got to be armed, don't you think?"

This was said in a more reasonable tone.

"Maybe, but what we have is out of all proportion to the threat. We don't need to be able to kill everyone on the planet several times over to be safe."

"There'll always be wars, though. Why should things change?"

"Because the weapons are so incredibly destructive now. Even if you *win,* you lose."

"Well anyway, how can that silly old bugger you were listening to last night do anything to stop wars? *How* old is he?"

"He'll soon be ninety-two."

"But why should anyone listen to *him,* at *that* age?"

"His age makes no difference. What matters is what he has to *say.*

And he isn't alone. There are plenty of other important thinkers… "

At that moment the Manager came in, bringing the debate to an end - just when I felt I had been making progress.

Over the next few weeks I made attempts to re-kindle the debate, but with out any success. Then, first thing one morning, to my amazement, one of the bigots actually took the initiative.

"I expected to hear more from you this morning, Brian."

"About what?"

"Your hero."

"Who's that, then?"

"Come on - *Bertrand Russell!*"

Everyone in the office had stopped working, I noticed.

"Oh… So what about him?"

"Didn't you watch the box last night?"

"No… Did I miss something?"

"Only the man *himself.*"

"I'm not with you."

"There was a *whole programme* about him. A full hour. Some kind of birthday tribute. Ninety-two, is he?"

I was the only one in the office to have missed it!

6
NADIR

But there were other arguments on other subjects. and one summer's day (though the season of the year was of course quite invisible in that office), after a particularly bruising clash with the "team" on the contentious issue of hanging (then still in full swing, as you might say), I was called in by the Manager (Mr Scroggins by name - or *something* Dickensian, at any rate) and warned that I was becoming a disruptive influence.

"But why pick on me?"

He glanced at the spy-window. "I don't miss much from here."

"It takes *two* to make an argument, though, surely?"

"From what I've observed it takes the *entire office.*"

"But I'm only one of half-a-dozen."

"Yes, and you seem to do more talking than the rest put together.

Lecturing them, by the look of it. Just who do you think you are?"

This was a searching and disturbing question. Did I see myself as a kind of poor man's Bertrand Russell, putting the world to rights at every opportunity?

"Only a humble draughtsman," I answered untruthfully.

"I'll thank you not to be sarcastic. The drawing office was a much quieter place before you came on the scene. So be warned - no more of it or you'll be down the road! That'll be all."

*

One reason I had missed the Bertrand Russell TV tribute was that I had a girlfriend in Liverpool just then - met at a dance. So I was doing a lot of travelling, in one way or another. Something had to give, and I started to reach work late, with increasingly threadbare excuses. As ever, though, I was a little slow to grasp that it was time once more to move on. Then it occurred to me that it would be damned convenient if I could find a *job* in Liverpool. So I casually bought a Liverpool evening paper to read on the train home - and I saw that they were advertising for a draughtsman (just one) at the Meccano factory, to design Dinky toys. Intrigued, I wrote to them, and was offered an interview.

It went far better than expected. I felt certain I was in. I even went so far as to confide in a colleague at Custom Refrigeration, who was the nearest I had to a friend there. (Or so I thought.) Then there was trouble with a light, narrow cabinet I'd designed. It had a drop-down door, and when you opened the door the thing pitched forward. Fell over, that is. It seems funny now, but didn't then. I was called into Scroggins' office for another chat. I hadn't yet had any word from Meccano.

"I hear you're thinking of leaving us," he said.

"Am I?"

"So I've heard on the grapevine."

"Oh, I see."

"It's time for you to sling your hook anyway, Darwent, with the way you've been performing."

"You mean I'm *sacked.*"

"To be kind, we'll call it redundancy. And while it's Friday afternoon, you can take the rest of the day off. Your wages and cards will be in the post. Don't bother coming back. Try the Labour Exchange in town. I'm sure they'll have something suitable for you there."

So without further delay I picked up my lunch-box and a few other belongings, went out to the bike shed, and rode slowly away from Custom Refrigeration, never to return.

*

Sitting on a bench in Albert Square, eating my usual cheese sandwiches, I wondered again if this might not be the moment for a career change.

There must surely be more stimulating jobs around than the ones I'd had to date. Nothing very sensible came to mind - I knew I was probably too old already to train as an airline pilot, and a bit lacking physically to be a lumberjack - but I resolved to pursue the possibilities with vigour at the Labour Exchange, before settling for another drawing-office job.

The large reception area had individual and rather plush cubicles, in which you could have a private, even intimate conversation. Nor did I have long to wait.

'What kind of work have you been doing?" asked the young lady who came to interview me.

"I'm a draughtsman."

She opened a drawer, which I could see was crammed with the usual well-thumbed job cards.

"But I could be looking for something different," I quickly added.

"Not very much for draughtsmen here, I'm afraid."

"No… Well, I'm willing, as I say, to consider something else. That's what I *want* to do, in fact… Something interesting, I hope. I do a bit of writing, and I'm quite a good artist. Could you give me an idea of what kind of alternative jobs might be available?"

'There are one or two contracting jobs here. Are you prepared to travel?"

"Perhaps. Yes."

"You don't sound very sure. Are you married?"

"Not yet," I grinned. "What kind of jobs are they?"

"For draughtsmen."

"But I've said I'm very willing to try something else. *Anything,* in fact, so long as the job is interesting."

"Well, the only jobs for draughtsmen are these contracting ones, as I say. Abroad… To be honest, they look a bit dubious to me. We've had them on our books for ages. But you could *try.*"

"What else have you got?"

"Nothing at all, really."

"What - no jobs of any description in the *whole of Manchester?* It's a wonder you manage to stay in business."

"None for *draughtsmen*... They're usually advertised in the papers, you know. Have you had a look there?"

"No, because I've decided that I don't want to *be* a draughtsman any more. I'm *sick* of it. I thought you might have something *else* to offer me."

"What other kind of engineering job could you do?"

"None. But I don't seem to be making myself clear. I want to get out of engineering *altogether,* into a *different field.*"

"I can't advise you there. I suggest you look in the press. Why not try the *Manchester Evening News?* They usually have one or two jobs for draughtsmen advertised."

"No thanks. The last job I got out of that paper was a *disaster.* And I moved on to something even worse."

"I'm sorry, but that's all I can advise. Good afternoon."

Standing on the steps, I looked up at the grey Manchester sky and thought it was just the setting for this new low point in my working life and times. The best you could say of the day so far was that it wasn't actually raining. Three weeks had now passed since my interview with Meccano, too, so there appeared little hope there... Well, it was only half-past-one, but there was nothing more I could do in Manchester so I caught an early train home, this time taking my bike with me. I had Bertrand Russell in my saddlebag, but I didn't attempt to read.

*

Arriving home before three, I was surprised to find the house empty. My mother had evidently gone shopping - maybe into town, so she could be gone for ages. Nor did I have a front-door key. I'd never bothered with one. There was a dark, dusty place in the shed where a back-door key was always kept, but when I groped for it I found it was missing. I went around to the front again and looked in through the window. I almost cried out, for there in full view, propped up on the mantelpiece, was a blue envelope, which I recognised as being from Meccano. My hopes soared… But how could I get in?

I couldn't stand and wait for my mother. I looked energetically around the small semi, but could find only one window open and that was too small for me to climb through. It was a window in the lean-to at the back of the house, always left open for ventilation over the gas cooker. I found a box to stand on and stuck my head through it. How bloody frustrating! Then I noticed another window that I had forgotten about - directly opposite on the far side of the lean-to. This one was big enough to climb in through. But it was on the latch. Damn!

Then suddenly I had a brainwave. What about the *clothes prop?* This was a device for raising a washing line - basically a long stick with a vee notch at one end. Maybe I could use it to stretch across and lever the latch off its peg.

It was just about long enough, and the latch lifted easily. So far so good. Now it was time to tap the window frame to open it, still using the prop. I knew I'd have to be careful, because the old lean-to was pretty ramshackle. But the first taps didn't work, so I tried a little harder, vaguely conscious that I had never seen this particular window open, and that it might well be glued up with paint… Still no good - but I simply had to get my hands on that letter… Soon I was hitting the window frame with all my might - up and down, round and round - when suddenly the *whole end* of the lean-to fell out.

No matter. I was *in!* I picked my way through the broken glass and other debris, and raced through to the front room. Tearing open the blue envelope, I read:

> *Further to your interview for a position with this company, I* am *writing to inform you that* we *hope soon to draw up* a *shortlist of suitable candidates.*

Sensing a movement outdoors, I glanced through the front window - and saw my mother hurrying up the front path with her shopping bag.

7
GOOD BEHAVIOUR

She would have been slow to recognise it, but my mother's life had been a life of work. A small, energetic woman, besides working six evenings a week as a barmaid, she had for years - going back to the days of wash tubs and hand-turned mangles - virtually run two households, following the tragic early death of her youngest sister. Her education had been pretty basic, but there had been small-business people in her family, so she was by instinct a working-class Tory. Despite never having in her life been paid more than a pittance, she believed that hard work and good behaviour were sure to be rewarded. She despised scroungers, and yet she was very indulgent when it came to my own failings - at least on the surface. She also had a good sense of priorities, so when she reached the front room, coming in by the same route as me, she said nothing about the damage to the lean-to.

"Why are you home so early?" she asked.

I outlined the day's events.

"I see." She put down her shopping bag and began removing her coat. "What does that letter say? Did you get the job?"

I handed it to her.

"Sounds as if they haven't even made up their minds whether they want anybody at all," she muttered.

I had to agree.

There was a pause. I knew she had every right to feel angry with me -well into my twenties now, and still struggling to find my place in the world. And *still* sometimes talking about being an artist - or even a *writer,* for God's sake! But all she said when she next spoke was:

"What time is it?"

She could see the clock as well as I could, but I answered:

"Quarter-to-four."

"Look, why not try the Labour Exchange in town? They'll be open till five, I should think."

"What? I've just been to that big Labour Exchange in Manchester. I *told* you. They don't *have* jobs for draughtsmen in those places. You've got to look in the *papers.*"

"Well, try the one in town, anyway. You never know."

"It would be a total waste of time."

"Just *try* them… I'll speak to your father later about the lean-to."

"But it's *hopeless.* And this *is* Friday afternoon as well, don't forget. doubt if they'll even *talk* to me."

"Just *try!*"

"I can't *face* it… I'll have a look in the evening papers, the same as usual."

"The papers haven't been much use to you so far, have they? Now go on!"

"There's more chance of finding a job in the papers than down at the Labour Exchange, believe me."

"You can look in the paper *afterwards,* can't you? Now get moving, before I lose my temper!"

"But I don't even know if I want to be a draughtsman anymore."

That did it.

"Don't start all *that* again! How long do you think it's going to take your father to fix that damage, working overtime most nights? Couldn't you have waited till I got in, instead of wrecking the place?"

"But I'll *help* him."

"*Hinder* him, more like. The pair of you will be having a row before you've knocked in the first nail. Now get down to the Labour Exchange this minute! And don't you *dare* come back here saying you got into an argument!"

Not for the first time, I sensed that living in the family home couldn't go on for much longer. I was a cuckoo in the nest! I sighed deeply, then got on my bike once more and pedalled slowly into town.

*

It was a little after four when I entered the familiar and depressing room. The man I approached - in a suit, and with Brylcreemed hair and a small moustache - seemed already to be shaking his head.

"Jobs for draughtsmen!" he laughed, interrupting me before I'd got through explaining myself- something that still annoys me intensely. "Not a hope! Have you tried the newspapers?"

"Not yet… Can't you just have a look?"

He checked his watch, then opened a drawer and began flicking through the usual cards, turning down the corners of his mouth and slowly shaking his head again as he did so.

I waited…

And then to my amazement he pulled out a card.

"They always want draughtsmen up at Power Hydraulics, of course," he said. "But I expect you've thought of them."

"Who?"

"Power Hydraulics."

The idea of reaching for his lapels, as in the films, crossed my mind.

But I remembered my mother's words and said politely:

"They want *draughtsmen,* did you say?"

"Of course, yes. They always do. We have a permanent card here, as a matter of fact… Do you know where they are?"

"Yes. Two hundred yards from where I live."

"What? I'm surprised you don't work there already!"

I didn't want to tell him that it was one of the companies where they offered real apprenticeships in proper engineering, that quite a few of my friends had gone to work there from school and then failed to progress to the Drawing Office, and that consequently I had always felt intimidated by the place.

"Do you really think they'd take me on?"

"Why not?"

"But surely they're extremely choosy, aren't they?"

"Oh, I wouldn't think so. They're always looking for people."

"Are you sure? *Power Hydraulics?*"

"Of course I'm sure."

I could hardly believe my ears. Could it conceivably be possible that I might be able to stroll around all that competitive shop-floor struggle and steal a prized drawing-office job from under my friends' noses - when I was as ignorant of real engineering as ever?

"Quite sure?"

"Yes."

"Absolutely sure?"

"Yes, *absolutely* sure."

I felt another rush of anger.

"Then why on earth were you so damned *negative* when I walked in here just now? I mean, *Jesus Christ!*"

The man glared at me for several seconds.

"Now look! Do you want me to arrange an interview for you, or shall I pop this card right back in the drawer and we'll forget all about it? It's up to you."

"Yes please," I said, adding a silent prayer of thanks for my mother's persistence.

*

I prepared for the important interview by studying - more intensely than ever - the few technical and reference books I had kept from my college days. I felt like a raw beginner. Once, at Modern Age, I had briefly tried my hand on a lathe, but that had only been to make a fancy brass poker handle. When it came to other machine tools - millers, shapers, grinders, jig-borers and so on - I was ignorant of everything except their names. I couldn't imagine how I would be able to cover up such a lamentable lack of pretty basic knowledge. Of course, safely in the Drawing Office, I wouldn't have to know how to operate a milling machine. But I would have to know what it was capable of. I might even have to give precise instructions to the tradesman, for all I knew.

And that wasn't my only worry. What about any stress calculations - determining by calculation if a component would be strong enough for its intended duty? Rule-of-thumb had been good enough in my career so far. That surely wouldn't do now. And when it came to *moving* parts how was I going to deal with *them?* I expected to be laughed out of the interview room.

But the first surprise was that there *was* no proper interview room. I had expected to have to face an aggressive panel, who would bombard me with unanswerable questions. Instead, I was taken along to the office of the Chief Draughtsman, the obese and amiable Bert Forest.

"I see you've worked at Modern Age," he remarked, after we'd got through the pleasantries." I'd had to fill in a form.

"Well, yes," I answered, expecting it to count against me. "But that *was* some time ago, sir."

"Only two or three years, surely?"

"It's nearer *six,* sir," I told him, exaggerating a little.

"Then the Merchant Navy... yes... but what *have* you been doing since then?"

"I thought the best thing to do was broaden my experience. Keep changing jobs pretty frequently... you know."

"It only mentions *two* jobs here."

"That's true. It didn't quite work out as planned, I'm afraid."

"I see. And would you want to be leaving *us* after six months?" "Oh no, sir. I'm ready to settle down now, believe me."

"That's good."

He got to his feet abruptly - or as abruptly as his bulk would allow - at that point, and stepped out into the Drawing Office proper. It was a huge place with six rows of boards, stretching into the middle distance. A moment later he came back with someone in tow.

"Geoff Fraser!" I exclaimed, standing up myself.

"Did you know this young man when you worked at Modern Age?" Mr Forest asked him. "He claims to have worked there himself once. It may have been before your time, from what he's been telling me."

"Brian? Certainly, yes. I believe he actually worked for me for a little while."

"And what did you think of him? He wants a job here."

My former colleague looked me up and down. "Well, I can't see that he's changed much - hasn't lost an arm or anything like that. So I'd recommend him, certainly."

Such kindness! My chief memory of the office at Modem Age was the belt mender, and all *that* nonsense.

Sinking back into his chair, Bert Forest asked:

"When can you start?"

"Well, I'd like to take a week's holiday first, if that's all right with you."

"Fair enough... Shall we say a week on Monday, then?"

"Thank you, sir," I said. 'That's fine."

There were handshakes all round, and that was that. The interview ordeal was over. Leaving Forest's office, I glimpsed another familiar face from Modern Age. And then to my real surprise - half way down the office - *Harold Major,* the old Chief Engineer at Modem Age. He it was who had opted for my urinal design over Jim McNulty's, of course, back in the mid- 1950s.

Walking the mere two-hundred yards back home, my step was light indeed. It was all inexplicable, but I had the strong sense of having come in from the cold.

*

My wage was to be two pounds more than at Custom Refrigeration, and my daily travelling time reduced by ninety-five per cent - at least! All very pleasant, but even so, once the joy had worn off, I started once again to feel that I had still to be found out. Life couldn't be this easy. There would surely be a price to pay, sooner or later.

And yet the office was equipped from end to end with draughting machines, too. Another bonus! I was given a board quite close to Harold Major, and assigned to the same section.

He wasn't the Section Leader, however, but only a humble checker, it turned out. I wondered what had happened to bring him down in the world. We had the job of designing special attachments for hydraulic lifting equipment.

In the early stages, I was so nervous that I could scarcely control the pencil. Luckily, my first few tasks were pretty simple. I believed it couldn't be very long, though, before I was given something I couldn't cope with - and *then* where would I be? As with engineers in the Merchant Navy, the draughtsman's culture required you to do everything you could to solve a problem yourself before swallowing your pride and seeking help. But the days stretched into weeks, and the dreaded moment of truth never seemed to arrive. My tasks were more difficult now, though they were still simple enough. I might have claimed that they were beneath my capabilities. I couldn't understand it. Was this really all that would be expected of me? It sometimes seemed to me that I had done more challenging work as a raw apprentice with Jim McNulty.

Since I had to communicate with Harold Major to have my work checked - and since discipline was pretty lax compared with the Parish-Spencer regime at Modern Age - there was scope for chatting.

"I can't ever remember being quite so nervous as I was on my first day here," I told him one day, as we leaned on our elbows over one of my drawings, spread out on his table.

"I can't think why."

"It seemed like my last chance. I could hardly hold the pencil."

"Good heavens, you should have more confidence in your ability! How do you think *I* felt when I came here a few years back? I was too nervous to pick the pencil *up*, never mind *use* it. I hadn't been near a drawing board in twenty-five years. *And* I was old."

This was a chance to enquire about his recent personal history, but I thought it best to wait.

"All the same, it was hard for me, too, you know." He knew a little of *my* recent past.

"But what about that wonderful training we gave you at Modern Age?"

"What about it?"

"Priceless, that's what!"

I almost laughed. "You've *got* to be joking!"

"Not me. Not these days. *Priceless,* I tell you."

"I've certainly never thought of it like that before. In fact I've always felt rather ashamed of it."

"You bloody fool! Any draughtsman who learned his trade under old Parish's nose has got a lot going for him. Ask Geoff Fraser over there. Or young Colin Whitbread. You can spot their work at a glance. What's more, you had the advantage of working with Jim McNulty. Now there was an artist and craftsman! By God!… He's still there, of course."

"What you're saying does start to make the casual interview I had with Bert Forest more understandable. I expected to be completely out of my depth, you know."

"Brian! You're one of the best draughtsmen I've ever come across. A *natural!* Even old Parish used to say so."

"Now that I *don't* believe."

"Oh yes. You were a rough diamond," he used to say. But full of promise."

"Come off it!"

"Those were his *exact words,* I tell you."

"Then how do you explain all the difficulties I've had with jobs? In interviews they turn their noses up at me. And Spencer wouldn't take me back when I left the Merchant Navy, you know. I wrote to him."

"Well, you can explain that for reasons I don't want to go into. Let's say the Drawing Office contracted pretty dramatically around that time. You probably wrote to him at the worst possible moment."

At that point Harold Major turned suddenly morose - something that would happen quite often in our time together at Power Hydraulics. "Poor you," he said finally. "Come and chat to me again when you have some *real* problems."

I thought afterwards that whatever had happened to him back at Modern Age must have been emotionally traumatic. It seemed to have affected his brain. No way had I been held in any kind of serious respect there, and his words about Jim McNulty struck me as over the top as well, much as I had admired the man's work. Then I talked one day to Colin Whitbread and got the story.

Not long after I left (spring, 1960), the company had been taken over by a financial conglomerate, and in short time -

something like the same morning - virtually the entire management purged. Harold Major had been among the victims. His chief crime was that he had been in the process of having a sailing boat made for himself in the Joiner's Shop. He had also had his house painted more than once by the firm's painters. An announcement had been made over the tannoy that those for the chop were to vacate their offices within the hour. Harold Major had passed through a far deeper Slough of Despond than I had experienced. Only religion had saved him. And even then he had had to rely on his worldly contacts, rather than on God himself, to find him a little job with Power Hydraulics.

*

I was with the company myself for nearly five years. I won't say that in that time I regained my confidence, because it had never been at a very high level. But I worked hard, steered clear of political arguments, read Bertrand Russell (and even the *Guardian)* in private, and generally behaved myself. I also gained valuable engineering experience, and in fact moved up to a sort of Assistant Section Leader. And I continued to hone my drawing-board skills, though sadly always conscious that Jim McNulty still remained supreme in that field.

Oh yes, and it was in that same period that I found the right girl at last. We were married in only a little more than a year. My old life as a Cuckoo in the Nest, groping for the back-door key in that dark place in the shed, was over. And before I moved on from Power Hydraulics, our first baby was on the way. In fact that was the reason why I left. I wasn't being paid enough to support a family alone. What's more, I had been hearing stories that there was a small fortune to be made if you grasped the nettle and went "contracting".

8
A DRAUGHTSMAN'S CONTRACTS

Working so close, it had been easy for me to have lunch with my mother at home, and this continued even after I was married. But now I scarcely knew where I was going to be at mid-day. It must have been a poignant moment for her - and she could never understand how anyone who *had* a job could contemplate moving elsewhere. For her generation that had been enough. But she made no complaint.

One amusing memory of that time is of taking my parents' young, energetic cairn terrier, Jock, for a walk at mid-day, after I'd eaten. The most economical way of doing it, I found, was to put him in the car and drive up to the railway bridge at the top of the lane. A straight, fenced path ran along the top of the cutting for about a quarter of a mile in both directions. It happened that the ten minutes I spent there coincided with at least two trains passing, and sometimes three. Jock soon developed a taste for chasing the trains along the path, and then for anticipating their arrival and beginning his run early. At the moment when the train caught up with him [this was in the days of steam, so there was plenty of noise) he appeared to experience a kind of frenzied climax. But he kept on chasing until it was out of earshot. And then, often without a pause, another train would approach from the other direction, so that he was compelled to repeat the procedure. The second train brought him right back to me, too. Driving home, poor Jock could only lie near an open window, exhausted but happy. "You're soon back!" my mother would comment. He lived to be fifteen, but he never lost his aggressive and adventurous spirit. We acquired a dog of our own eventually - Bob, a cross-bred Welsh collie. He would leap into your arms when he heard thunder. Jock used to run across the fields towards it, jumping at the sky and barking furiously, lightning flashing around him.

*

Ah well... My new employers, Technical Designs, had a small drawing office on their premises in town, but it was rare to find anybody actually working there. They much preferred to have their people working on the client's premises, bringing in the cash. The office was mainly somewhere to hang around until a job came up.

Not much effort was made to match a draughtsman to a specific job, for the reason that, as promised, the money was very good and the man would therefore make damned sure he performed well regardless of his suitability. That was also the reason why the agency wasn't particularly discriminating when it came to recruitment policy. They knew they could push almost anybody in at the deep end, and with the money incentive, sure enough he would bob to the surface and somehow swim.

There was no immediate contract for me, however, but I wasn't too worried because at the interview the Manager had said that rather than lay people off they were prepared to keep them occupied in the office, "polishing doorknobs", until something turned up. I spent my first few days doing menial tasks - lifting and carrying rather than polishing - though at nearly a pound an hour, and twelve months before I'd get my first tax bill, I wasn't inclined to complain about the indignity of it. Crossing the street each morning to enter the office, I used to smile at the large brass plate on the wall proclaiming that

Technical Designs could undertake anything from nuclear submarines to full chemical plants, as I seem to recall. And inside the only design resource was *me!*

Well, on my third day a job came in - though it would mean working in the office- and was aimed in my direction. It involved designing a new heating system for a small two-storey office block. Heating and ventilating expertise was listed on the sign (towards the bottom, low-tech end) but it was nevertheless a totally new field for me.

Still, the office did possess a catalogue of radiator designs, so that was a start. And while I hadn't a clue about relating the heat output of a radiator to the heat required to keep a room of a certain size warm, it wasn't rocket science to guess that a smallish room would need only a single radiator, and a somewhat bigger one probably two - right up to a conference room, for which four or five might be about right. Luckily, someone else was looking after the boiler installation. I only needed to lead the pipes to the blank corner rectangle shown on the plan.

In spite of my uncertainties, I was able to produce a drawing of a system that at least *looked* competent - half the battle to survive in this game, I would soon realise - with radiator capacities listed, along with other snippets of technical information I'd managed to cobble together. I sent it off to the client and waited for a response. A telephone call duly came, asking me to call in their office for a chat. I reported to reception and the girl contacted the man I'd been asked to see. Then she left the desk - only to return carrying a large brown envelope.

"It's all in here," she said, smiling. "Self-explanatory, he says. Nothing to worry about. OK?"

I left the building with a feeling of relief that my mission had been so easily accomplished. But before driving off, I thought I'd better take a look at his comments. I discovered that my drawing had been covered in incomprehensible, bad-tempered scribble. It meant nothing to me. I swallowed hard, and went back inside.

"I'm sorry," I said at the desk, "but I can't make head or tail of these instructions. I really do need to see the man. Could you ask if he'll give me five minutes."

"Well, I'll try. But I rather doubt it."

"Tell him it's *essential,* please."

The man turned out to be at least partly human, for he agreed to see me. He was about my own age, which was also a help. For once the draughtsman's code of not asking questions had to be broken.

"Look," I confessed, "this is all guesswork, as far as I'm concerned. These agencies take on jobs without ever thinking if they've got anyone competent around to carry them out."

"I'm afraid that's your worry. We only gave the job to you people to get it out of the way. If I've got to spend time on it, there's no point."

"Is it urgent?"

"Very."

I saw my chance.

"You do understand heating systems yourself, I take it?"

"Of course I do, yes. And in the case of your drawing I hardly knew where to begin… I'm afraid I rather lost my temper."

"Well, there's only one way that this job will ever be finished quickly, and that's by a bit of honest collaboration. You're wasting time pushing the job back at me… It shouldn't take us long… "

He was considerably taken aback by this audacious approach, but pretty soon we were going quietly through the necessary amendments.

And that's how I managed to bring the first of my contracting jobs to a satisfactory conclusion. I hurried straight back to Technical Designs' office, rapidly drew up a new plan in accordance with the client's helpful guidance, re-submitted it, and after clearing up a few further points my work was accepted and the agency paid.

But it wouldn't always be quite so easy.

*

Immediately after the heating job, I had the news that a draughtsman was needed at a big glass-making company. This seemed more like it. I was to report to a man named D'Oliviera. No interview was required - the company was a regular client, and Technical Designs already had a number of people dotted about the various offices. I was given a hint of a warning, though, that the tasks they were asked to undertake could be pretty bizarre. Still, they were very reliable payers.

I arrived promptly on Monday morning, as instructed, and was soon sitting opposite Mr D'Oliviera in his office. It was autumn, and the morning was an especially fine one. He had a panoramic view from his window of expanses of green lawn, a few trees, and a sprinkling of golden leaves. He asked where I had been on holiday that year, and I told him the Loire Valley. He had also visited the *châteaux,* so we compared impressions.

This year he had been to the Costa del Sol with his children. They were growing up now, he said, and would soon wish to holiday without their parents - a sad moment, didn't I think? I sympathised, telling him that for me all that still lay happily in the future. This pleasant chat went on for about twenty minutes, the sun streaming through the window, when he suddenly asked:

"What is it that you want exactly?"

I gulped, then showed him my credentials and reminded him gently that he had asked to see *me.*

He looked up at the ceiling, and stroked his chin. An embarrassing silence followed, during which I attempted to concentrate on the view. His mental processes were almost audible. Slowly, a glimmer of memory seemed to return to him.

"I remember making the phone call now," he said. "Last Monday or Tuesday, it would be... Now, what for?"

"Would it help to ask somebody?" I suggested.

"It might." He picked up his phone and summoned someone to his office. A lady appeared.

"Do you remember why we asked this young man from Technical Designs to come in today, Mrs Page?" he asked.

The secretary looked thoughtful. "I know it came after last week's meeting on maintenance procedures," she said. "Does that help?"

"By God, yes!" he exclaimed. "*Now* I remember. Come with me!"

I expected to follow him along corridors, and at last into a drawing office of some sort, but instead he slipped through a small side door, and we were on the works. Passing through a number of strange departments, we finally reached a small office hidden away in a dark corner. Entering, I saw two men in overalls, drinking tea and eating toast while they read their papers.

"This is where you will be working," said Mr D'Oliviera, introducing me briefly to my new colleagues. And with that he left.

The two men - one only a little older than me by the look of it, and the other closer to retirement age - appeared less than pleased to have their peace and comfort disturbed. They poured me a mug of tea and offered a piece of toast. To begin with they weren't inclined to enlighten me as to my duties. But they turned out to be a friendly pair - by nature very chatty- so I soon got the gist of why I was there.

The older man was a plumber, the younger a fitter. They each had a regular maintenance routine to carry out. That was all that their work consisted of. The problem (for the company) was that they carried what they did around in their heads. Lately, there had been pressure to have their routines written down and put into some kind of order. This was an idea they seemed to resent - for reasons that I couldn't yet fathom. They had refused point blank to cooperate with a member of staff, but had agreed to the compromise of having someone from outside undertake the task. That was to be my job. I'd be spending the next three weeks with them.

What they didn't tell me, and I found out from others, was that the pressure had arisen because the older man had recently had a serious heart attack and it was felt that he might soon have another, while the younger one had been involved in a bad motor-cycle accident, as a consequence of which he had been clinically dead for longer than the recommended four minutes.

But in spite of these misfortunes they were an engaging pair. The fitter's speech was a little slurred and his reaction time slightly delayed, while the plumber had always been a slow mover, I gathered. But they had a refreshingly philosophical attitude towards life. Having been as close to permanent death as anyone could get without actually being buried, they could now cheerfully face anything. Certainly, their duties at work were of small importance to them except as a means of earning a living. Not that they were incompetent. They were simply devoid now of ambition and the competitive spirit. In their private home-from-home they enjoyed life as best they could. They knew they had a strong moral advantage over their employers, and that as long as they were able to stay alive they couldn't really be touched.

Each day I followed one or other of them around the works while they oiled pump motors, checked lavatory flushings, and so on, making detailed notes. Towards the end of the third week I was able to draw up a large, multi-coloured chart, which showed at a glance what they did on a daily, weekly or monthly basis. The chart was gratefully received by Mr D'Oliviera. It gave no hint, however, of the strange inner lives of my two amiable friends.

*

So it was back to the office in town, where a job that had evidently been around for some considerable time had surfaced once more. It consisted of a small cardboard box, containing a variety of tiny clockwork wheels and spindles. The origins of this box of tricks had become a little obscure. It tended to be brought out as a kind of last resort in sluggish times. So far as anyone knew, the object had been to design a special machine that would automatically assemble the spindles with the wheels. They were a force-fit, so the thing would have to be pneumatically operated. But any information regarding which spindle went with which wheel was lost, together with how far along the spindle the wheel should be positioned - or for that matter whether it was several wheels to a spindle. The only thing known for certain was that the machine must not cost more than £500.

The name of the client was on file, but he could not be contacted for fear of awakening his interest in the job and thereby precipitating a demand for quick action. A credible scheme was required first, in the hope of convincing him that a genuine, competent effort had been put into the assignment. Payment for that might then be forthcoming, even if the machine was no longer wanted.

Several people passing through the office en route to a new outside contract had had this curious task pushed under their noses, but no one so far appeared to have got much beyond staring blankly into the box and perhaps shaking the parts about a bit. Not even a Leonardo-style freehand sketch, showing how the machine might look in simple terms, had ever been committed to paper. Now it was my turn to have a go. I wasn't going to be alone, however. Another recent recruit was also hanging about the office, so the Manager had the bright idea that we should devise competitive schemes. Not that there would be any *real* contest. This was in truth little more than another variation on polishing doorknobs.

The rival schemes as they emerged had distinct Heath-Robinson qualities, for neither of us had any experience of pneumatic machinery. Our different approaches simply reflected our different backgrounds. Mine must have betrayed evidence of my work up to that time, with odd fragments of the sort of components I'd designed at Modern Age or Power Hydraulics finding their way into my scheme and performing bizarre, even imaginary functions. I doubt if either machine could ever have been built, let alone used. But that was really beside the point. Technical Designs now had the basis for a fresh approach to the nearly forgotten client. I'd like to think that they were ultimately paid - at least *something*. Neither scheme, incidentally, was ever declared the winner. So far not so good in my new life as a contract draughtsman. The doorknobs were beckoning once more - but then good fortune suddenly smiled on me again in the shape of a prospective job at British Chemicals, one of the most important companies in the land.

9

LAST FRUSTRATIONS

This latest and last contract took me back to the normal atmosphere of life in a large drawing office. I had by now lost most of my fear of being unable to cope with the unfamiliar, but in such orthodox surroundings I expected to be given pretty mundane work again.

It was not to be. Knowing absolutely nothing about chemical-plant instrumentation, I was immediately assigned to the Instruments Section, a vacancy having occurred there. But thankfully the task my predecessor had begun, and which I now had to pick up, required no real technical expertise - only an ability to read the labels on the instruments dotted all over the plant, and to relate these to corresponding labels in the control room. Not that the job didn't present certain difficulties.

The instruments - flow control valves, alarms, trips, and so on - were actuated by compressed air, and the problem was that the compressed- air pipe *system,* serving several individual plants, had grown haphazardly over a long period, and had in a word become a shambles. No one any longer understood it, even though the instruments which relied on the air were still miraculously receiving their life-giving supply. The chemicals under control were dangerous, and it had sensibly been decided that this state of affairs would no longer do. A complete new ring main had therefore been installed, with tapping-in points at intervals. What was now needed was a plan to connect the infinitely complicated present system into the new main.

Obviously, the first step would be to do a drawing of this present shambles of a system, and in fact my predecessor had put months of effort into it already. He had produced a three-dimensional isometric line drawing on a single sheet of paper that was so complex that it was impossible to follow the lines. Here and there it was close to becoming just a black mass. In short he had driven the job into a corner, and then walked away from it. Hence the sudden vacancy in the office.

Each day I took his drawing out onto the plant and tried to check it against what actually existed. It was very difficult to follow, but I soon found his work was inaccurate in places, and incomplete. In fact some of it appeared to be sheer guesswork. What could I do? I surely couldn't abandon all the labour he had put in and start afresh, could I? Think of the months of work - and pay! Yet his drawing was far beyond correction. I dithered for a while, trying to add or correct a bit here and there. But it was no use. No *wonder* he'd scarpered! At length I had no choice but to present the difficulty to the engineer I was working for. It would mean a completely fresh start, and might ultimately require as many as half-a- dozen interlocking plans, I believed, so complex was the system.

"Fine," he said, after I had nervously outlined my proposal. "Suits me. Take your time with it, because we've got to get it right. And don't worry!"

This was my first insight into the difference between a large, multi-national company like British Chemicals, and the petty-minded smaller firms I'd been used to. The job took me a further four months, resulting in no less than *ten* separate isometric drawings. But at last I could devise a plan to simplify the present shambles and link it, bit by bit, into the new main. This finally happened, without a hitch. But at no stage had there been the kind of hysterical panic I might have expected, and no hint of a reproach that my labours had taken an inordinate length of time. The job in fact had gone well, everybody said.

*

It was rare at British Chemicals for a contract draughtsman to be brought in to do a specific job, as I had been. They tended to be used in a more general way, to make up the numbers. I wasn't sure what would happen to me when I had sorted out the instrument-air system, but in the event I was taken on more permanently - perhaps because I had demonstrated the qualities of doggedness and reliability which working on a chemical plant in an essentially care-and-maintenance role demanded. The work wasn't exactly enjoyable, but then I hadn't yet begun to think of work in terms of enjoyment. Aged thirty now, all I knew was that I had no wish to return to the crazy world of the contract draughtsman, as it were, on the loose.

I wasn't looking for much more than a reliable continuation of the good wages I was earning as a contract draughtsman (we now had a baby daughter), though I'd begun to notice other positive things about this new working environment. Because with a big operation time scales were inevitably much longer, decision making could generally be more relaxed, with time for proper discussion - and even exchanging ideas. I had of course been more or less told what to do in the past. It all added up to a more civilised and democratic approach to work. Even so, the chemical industry was still pretty unpromising territory for someone who remained at heart an artist, writer and an amateur philosopher.

The role of the draughtsman based on site, caught up in mundane tasks such as minor modifications or improvements, was not a glamorous one. Not for him the clean and tidy work of the off-site man - designing tor greenfield situations, with fresh, reliable reference drawings to hand, in a warm, carpeted office, and scarcely any need to visit the site at all. Instead, in all weathers - just as I had done with the instrument-air job - he would have to trudge great distances, scale ladders and clamber over old pipes and steelwork, to check on and measure what actually existed, as opposed to what the old, out-of-date drawings indicated should really be there. Only then could he begin to design afresh.

And he would do all this knowing full well that such tedious labour was barely acknowledged, never mind respected, by the senior people. Meanwhile the draughtsman who could sit in his pleasant office for most of the time, with everything he needed to hand, would earn more Brownie Points, and hence move more smoothly up the salary ladder. This was in part because he would be responsible for spending larger sums of money. That tended to be what counted.

Setting forth on his frequent visits to the plant, the site draughtsman would cut something less than a dashing figure. As a minimum in special or protective clothing, he would be obliged to wear a brown, coat-type overall, and balance on his head (adjusting them was always difficult) a heavy safety helmet, with goggles attached for lowering when needed.

If the weather was cold (which was often the case, for chemical plants could be chilly places), a thick donkey jacket would be worn over the longer brown overall. Gloves, too, or sometimes big protective gauntlets, would also be worn against the cold. And then, depending on where he was bound, he might well have rubber over-shoes over his own footwear, or even safety boots. If he was likely to enter an area where gas escapes might occur, he would be further lumbered with a gas mask, in a canvas shoulder bag. And occasionally a torch might be needed, or a Polaroid camera. Always, too, he would have with him his sketch pad, pens and pencils, and finally his trusty folding wooden rule.

Thus kitted out and weighed down, as he made his way along the office corridors to reach the works, he would be unlikely to attract many wolf whistles from the typists and mail girls.

Even so, some site draughtsmen, especially those who had grown up in the chemical industry, seemed to secretly love the plant. Standing in the midst of its soaring towers, vessels and steel structures, deafened by noise and with a whiff of unpleasant substances in the air, they felt that this was what it was all about. Forget drawings, offices, telephones, meetings, *people* - all the things that had gone into its creation, and still contributed to keeping it in efficient running order. What mattered in the end was the plant itself, the monstrous money-earner, Drawings would be filed away. People would move on to other jobs, retire, even die. The plant was the only reality.

But not for me.

Jim McNulty was I'm sure ultimately to blame, but my finer feelings, in so far as they were aroused, lingered at the design stage. I was willing to confront the plant, grapple with it, almost weep over it at times, above all acknowledge it as my final source of livelihood. But I could never have reverential feelings towards such a thing. For its permanence was in fact an illusion. Chemical plants do not have long lives. From within, they are under relentless corrosive attack. They rust, become ugly, and ultimately, if they are not demolished, turn into monstrous eyesores. New products emerge and demand changes. Chemical plants become obsolete, or redundant. They have never been an unchanging part of the universe. Drawings of them can in fact have far more permanence, and they are certainly prettier to look at.

*

At British Chemicals I for the first time encountered graduate engineers. I was of a generation unused to thinking much about universities. I had gone to grammar school, but the question of going on to university had been little mentioned. This was probably because the number of people qualifying had to match the places then available, and that was before the expansion of the university system in the 1960s and '70s. Only the best people made it, and they needed parents who understood such things. I wasn't a contender. Nor did it ever bother me.

Instead, it had left me with the vague notion that universities were essentially for studying Latin and Greek. And throughout my working life so far I had only worked with people who had come up as I had through the technical-college system. But now I was finding that there existed an engineering elite - people who had studied the subject at university and had leapt far ahead up the grades and salary ladder. In fact university graduates automatically came into the company at a higher level than a technical-college man might ever hope to reach, while draughtsmen like myself, who might have imagined they were doing pretty well in the engineering game, were discovering that a Higher National, which they may have imagined represented the highest attainment in engineering scholarship, in fact meant next to nothing. Of course, as a contracting agency man still, I stood somewhat apart from this. Later, on the staff myself, whenever I challenged the system I was told that the company was immensely profitable, so it obviously worked. In fact these people attributed the company's success directly to their own superior qualities and vital contribution.

I possessed only an *Ordinary* National, but joining the staff after about eighteen months proved surprisingly easy. Contract people at British Chemicals had seasons of favour, though at the same time they lived under a sort of cloud. The advantage of employing them was that they could be quickly dispensed with when difficult times came. So they were useful. But, rather better paid as they were than staff people, they could be resented, as well as being seen as motivated solely by money, with no genuine or ongoing interest in the work as such. This all made for uneasy working relations and periodic demands that contractors - some had been around for years - should join the staff or go. When the chance came, I found myself ready to make the move. It was effectively by the back door. Had I made a direct application to the company, I doubt if I would even have been called in for interview.

*

So things were certainly going rather better now - but there is one thing I haven't yet mentioned. The office was *not* equipped with draughting machines. The boards did have a broad straight edge, mounted on a pulley system, with a stiffening rib which, when the drawing board was tilted, served as a handy shelf for odds and ends, but your set-square and scale rule were still loose items. For me this antiquated equipment was a major irritation, so I began raising the issue at our office monthly meetings. But the mood was against me.

These draughting machines don't sound very suitable for chemical-plant work," said one colleague. "I've got to be able to draw a horizontal line right across the drawing, from one side to the other. That wouldn't be possible, from what you say."

"And where," said another, "would you put your compasses, rubber, cigarettes, and other loose stuff?"

"Anyway," added a third (this man actually a section leader), "even if you *could* draw any faster, all it would mean is that you'd begin rubbing the lines out again that much *sooner,* wouldn't you? Changes are always needed, in my experience. Nothing is ever right first time."

They all nodded to that one. And when I said I believed that using a draughting machine would add about five years to your life span, I was laughed at.

But, with the vague support of only one other man, I was persistent, so to shut me up it was decided that a single draughting machine should be acquired for assessment purposes. Those who wanted to could have a go with it, and more *might* be obtained if it proved popular. But if it got the general thumbs down, that would very definitely be that.

Of course I fully expected that the machine would be fitted to *my* drawing board, but I was informed that I was completely biased, and so it was given instead to the other man who had shown lukewarm interest. He was pleased, and enjoyed using it, but few others could be bothered "-- to sit in his chair and at least get the feel of it. The overwhelming verdict was unmistakably negative.

I was gobsmacked, as we say these days. I could so easily see the years stretching ahead, through which I was going to be labouring with the present equipment. I was convinced that it really *would* shorten my life. In desperation, I confided in the graduate engineer I was working for- and it must have been almost a sob story, for he told me he had a little money left in his budget, and was prepared to use it to purchase a draughting machine for me. It was a highly unorthodox proposal, which led to a battle royal with the Chief Draughtsman (only a technical-college man), but with common sense on his side the engineer won the day. In fact when the machine duly arrived I received an office cheer. I did my best to smile.

*

Soon afterwards I moved on from general plant work into a line involving special-purpose equipment. This was closer to what I had been used to in the past, and decidedly more interesting, giving me the chance even to be a little inventive - a rare privilege. But my new engineer and I were not exactly hitting it off. He was an energetic, stimulating character, but not a believer in hands-off management. On the contrary, he enjoyed standing at my shoulder giving me instructions, while I merely pushed the pencil. I could understand why the full job title of "draughtsman" had in earlier times been *"engineer's* draughtsman". I used to feel that if I were to move away for a moment, he would take over.

He could also be unreasonably critical. I was confident enough by now to know when I was right, and even in a subordinate role to insist on it. But we had some pretty fierce arguments, with the rest of the office as audience. The clashes got worse and worse, and there's no telling what the outcome might have been had his work not petered out.

So that's where I was in the late summer of 1975 - thrown back into the general pool, and still as far away as ever from finding the right home for my temperament and talents. To expect such a thing seemed like a fantasy. My career might even nose dive, for we were moving into a new technological age, with computers just starting to make an appearance in offices, and far from embracing these changes, I saw them instead as an unwelcome intrusion. But with another baby on the way there was no possibility of my turning my back on the salary and conditions available at British Chemicals. It looked as if I would simply have to be prepared for a long, hard slog - until the blessed day of retirement at last arrived.

But mercifully that was not to be.

One day, out of the blue, the Chief Draughtsman's phone rang and a voice asked:

"Do you happen to have a good development designer working in your office?"

Before he could stop himself, for he was neither a friend nor admirer of mine, he blurted out:

"Yes, Brian Darwent. Why?"

But the caller already had the confirmation he wanted.

*

It emerged that the engineer I had been in the habit of quarrelling with had been talking to a graduate engineer working on another site, who had been appointed to the task of developing a vital new process that would require entirely new hardware that could be manufactured using mass-production methods. He needed as a partner a designer with flair, conceptual skills, the ability to present ideas graphically, and the maturity to work alone for much of the time.

My old adversary - fearing perhaps that we might one day have to work together again - had enthusiastically recommended me for the post.

*

But there were two battles still to come - one minor, one major.

Firstly, the Chief Draughtsman - who had till now thought of me as a square peg, and at times a damned nuisance - now suddenly claimed that I was a vital asset to the office, calling me in for a private chat to tell me this. I was forced to argue that, on the contrary, I had never fitted in and found it remarkable that I had been taken on the staff. It was a very weird kind of debate, with no winner - but the engineer who was seeking to recruit me cut through all this and demanded that I be let go. If not, he said he would take it to a higher level. So I was reluctantly given my freedom.

The other issue concerned my precious draughting machine, and this battle was more ferocious.

Expecting little opposition, I knocked on the Chief Draughtsman's door to ask if he would mind if I took it with me - the drawing board and draughting machine combined. His first name was Charles.

"*What?*" he said. He was practically speechless. "No you bloody well can not!"

"But why, for goodness' sake?"

"Because *I* say you can't."

"But no one else wants it. You know how negative everyone felt on the issue. It will only end up being dumped somewhere. And I do really need it for my new work."

"Forget it! I'm *not* letting you have it."

"It doesn't even strictly *belong* to this office, you know - if you recall how it was purchased."

"Well it belongs here *now*. It certainly doesn't belong to *you*. And you're *not* taking it with you. It's an *outrageous* idea. Suppose *everybody* claimed to have their own fancy drawing board and expected to lug it around the company whenever they moved to a new office! Now get back to your board and get some bloody work done for a change! You haven't left us *yet*, you know."

I sat at my board for a while. Then I approached my section leader, hoping for *his* support. I told him the tale, in a reasonable way.

"I'm in full agreement with Charles," he said. "It's quite ridiculous that you should imagine the board belongs to *you*. For the last time, it's staying right *here*. Now get on with your work!"

But persistent as ever, I thought of another approach. We were all in a union. It wasn't a militant union - far from it. In fact the stewards felt very underused. More than that, they had recently been quietly touting for business, as you might say, looking for an issue they could maybe get their teeth into.

I doubted if my little drawing-board grievance really deserved their attention, but I telephoned our local man and he suggested a quiet chat. The draughting machine was indeed a minor issue, he explained, but far more serious was the strong likelihood that I would now be leaving under a cloud. That would be unfair and undeserved. He said he would raise the matter with the General Services Manager, Mr Tasker. This man was an ex-military, no-nonsense type. He was also Charles's boss.

Despite the docile nature of our particular union, at that time the unions in general were starting to flex their muscles. The general policy of the company was to avoid trouble. So I wasn't altogether surprised when, a few days later, Mr Tasker's secretary summoned me to his office.

I very much feared a dressing down, military style, but the man was unusually warm and friendly. I explained my point of view yet again. He seemed sympathetic, rather to my surprise. Then he picked up his phone.

"Charles," he said. "I understand there's an issue with Brian Darwent. He's leaving us soon. Will you come down, please."

Charles duly arrived, rather breathless - and clearly shocked to find that I was ahead of him. I was occupying the only available spare chair, too, so he had no option but to remain standing.

"Now, what's all this about?" said his boss, in a soothing tone. "Brian tells me he'd like to take his drawing board to his new job. I believe it's got some sort of special attachment that he'd find useful… Is there a problem with that?"

'Well, yes, there is. It isn't *his,* you know."

"But he isn't leaving the company, is he? He isn't planning to take it *home* with him… Does someone else in the drawing office want to use his special board, by chance?"

"Not exactly, no."

"Well, then, I think you should allow him to take it with him. Let's say as a goodwill gesture. Is that all right?"

"I still don't like the idea, Mr Tasker. What if *everybody*… "

"But it's only *Brian,* isn't it?… Now, I really *do* think you should listen a little more closely to the needs of your staff, Charles."

Mr Tasker turned to me.

"Is that all right with you, then, Brian?"

"Fine, yes - thanks," I said, trying not to smile.

"Now, I want there to be no further bad feelings between you two. We can't have Brian departing under a cloud. I want you both to leave this office together, and to shake hands outside. All right?"

Charles was first to the door. I turned to give the General Services Manager a final nod of appreciation.

'Thank you, sir," I heard myself say, just stopping short of a salute.

By the time I'd closed the door behind me, Charles was legging it down the corridor.

10
HOME AND DRY

I won't say that my working life was instantly transformed in my new job. I always disliked the upheaval of change, and found settling into a new routine more irritating than stimulating. And wasn't I working on a drawing board still, inside the chemical industry? I might have an office to myself now, but what else was new? Only slowly did I wake up to the fact that I had indeed found my right and rightful home at long last.

The *work* was new. Anyone unfamiliar with life in industry might think that all design work is new, though nothing could be further from the truth. Everything I had ever designed on the drawing board until then had been strongly linked to something already well-established. Always it amounted only to a kind of tinkering. This was a way of life that suited the majority of draughtsmen. If they couldn't find a precedent to build upon they were apt to be lost. My temperament ran counter to that. I preferred working without reference to anything that had gone before. It wasn't that I was seeking a challenge - in fact I sometimes felt I was being lazy, for I never had the patience to dig into old files and follow up something that was vaguely similar. No, for whatever reason, I never felt happier than when I was designing a thing from scratch. And that was precisely what would now be required of me.

Another pleasure was that for the first time I began to have a large measure of control over my working day. I could often decide for myself how best to overcome problems or obstacles - whom to talk to, whether to visit another site, or a subcontractor. Not that I found this easy at first. The belief that my primary function was to work on the board, and that time spent away from it amounted to slacking, was so deeply ingrained that I had quite a job wrestling with the guilt. It seemed astonishing that I was free to jump in my car and visit a firm doing work for us - a visit that would usually include lunch. Regardless of how justified my trip had been, I would fear as I re-entered the site that armies of workmen might appear, brandishing crude weapons, and come running to drag me from my car and lynch me for being a parasite. But soon enough I became adjusted to that side of the job.

Maybe the most surprising thing - working in a new field - was that I could continue to get by with little in the way of technical or scientific knowledge. But that was where working for a big company was a huge advantage. In smaller firms, draughtsmen would have to grapple, often under pressure, with mind-numbing technical problems themselves. But companies like British Chemicals had all the relevant specialists in-house, so the draughtsman in such circumstances was never stuck tor someone to consult if he had a technical difficulty. In fact he hardly ever needed to open a reference book himself.

It might be thought that, even in the late '70s, a draughtsman who l_ knew nothing about computers, and was making no attempt to acquaint himself with them, would soon be struggling. Already there were people who were saying that draughtsmen wouldn't be needed tor much longer, since it would all be done with computers. Well, the answer to that was that it was the *draughtsmen* of course who would have to *operate* them. Meanwhile the threat to the older methods, especially at the conceptual stage of a project, wasn't as yet really very serious.

*

We had seven or eight great years - the best by far of my whole working life. I was a happy man. The company was still prodigiously wealthy and profitable. We were engaged in Research and Development work, and it was well-supported. (More than that, the company had to be seen by the financial markets to be spending a certain proportion of its profits on R&D, or its share price might suffer.) I was deeply involved in one highly successful project and looked forward to others. I was making strides up the salary ladder. And it was in that happy period that I honed my skills to the point where I was at last fully satisfied with the style and execution of my work. It had taken a long time. CAD (computer-aided-design) might be starting to encroach, but I felt confident I was the best draughtsman around - by some distance.

And then things started to happen. I thought it was very significant that the term "Research and Development" was replaced by "Research and Technology". The idea of *development-* our essential bread and butter - was subtly downgraded. A new mentality was emerging which saw *technology* as the answer to everything. "Why do we have to bother with all this costly and time-consuming development nonsense?" was the question on certain people's lips, "when technology has all the answers now." And this conveniently coincided with a necessary scaling back of cash for development funding.

Having managed to weather the recession of the early '80s, by the end of the decade the company was in serious trouble. Development funding dried up altogether. Instead, there was a call for volunteers for early retirement. Almost *anybody* could go. The terms on offer - wafted under our noses - were extraordinarily generous. Whatever had brought about this state of affairs, the university graduates who had claimed that they were the reason for the company's success in the good times now could only respond by joining the early-retirement queue. The company was belatedly following much of the rest of our manufacturing industry - either downsizing or disappearing. It would now be up to the financial sector to earn the nation's wealth.

I lasted until 1994, and then limped on as a contract draughtsman again for a few more years. I still had my draughting machine, and was still using it. I never touched a computer. One of the last jobs I did was a series of complex, three-dimensional, exploded assembly drawings of certain of our products. My original drawings were then scanned and transferred to a computer. It was then possible to painstakingly replace my pencil lines, one by one, with computer-generated lines (someone else of course did all this), so that the final image was indistinguishable from a computer drawing, and ready for printing in a servicing manual. That was as near as I got to a compromise.

For I remained a pencil-on-paper man to the bitter end - inspired all those years ago by Jim McNulty. He never ceased to be the hero of my working life. I had known draughtsman vastly more knowledgeable than Jim, but no one who could begin to match him in the business of using a beautifully-sharpened pencil to put straight lines, curves, circles and printed words on a sheet of drawing paper to such wonderful artistic effect. No one, that is, except - just possibly - myself.

AND NOW …

I'm now looking back more than twenty years to my working life and wondering what became of all the places where I once earned my living, and of course of my work colleagues. I live too far away and I'm too old at eighty-one to do much investigating. I last did that ten years ago.

Modern Age, rather surprisingly, still existed. The imposing red-brick office frontage, which I first saw in the late 1940s, was still there. Standing outside the main office entrance, it would have been easy for me to go in with some excuse, and perhaps see once more the precise spot where I had that exceedingly awkward encounter with Gillian Wade. But I held back.

What happened to her? I once glimpsed her in town, but we didn't speak. In fact she didn't *see* me. Still too timid, I made sure of that. It would have been in the late '50s. How is her exquisite profile looking today? She would have been a year or two older than me, so she'll be further into her eighties than I am.

As for the Maintenance Drawing Office, as it was below ground level I couldn't tell if it still existed, or even be sure which window it would have been as they were all the same from the outside. And Jim McNulty himself, what about him? He was roughly the same age as my dad, so he would be a hundred-and-fifteen today. How long did that tuft of hair last? He had a son, then aged only six. The boy will be seventy now. Jim survived the purge, unlike of course Harold Major, who I now remember wrote me a flattering reference, which may well have been crucial in my getting into the Merchant Navy in the nick of time, thereby escaping the dreaded National Service.

When I was having a look at the office frontage, I had a peer over an adjoining fence and saw that the roof of the Design Office, some distance away, was all caved in. I presumed it had either been abandoned or was in the process of being demolished. Old Mr Parish must surely have passed away ages ago. Spencer, I've heard, died of a heart attack. Bill Collins vanished totally from my life when I left the company, as of course did the poor belt mender.

It's a long time since I drove down Liverpool's old Dock Road, though I did discover that the dock where the *Pizarro* used to berth was still in existence, albeit empty of course of vessels. How different it all looked back in 1960-61. I didn't imagine my Merchant Navy life had touched me emotionally, but twenty years later, watching the final episode of *Boys from the Blackstuff,* I felt quite upset. You may remember Yosser Hughes pushing the sad old union guy, dying of cancer, around the empty docks in a wheelchair. It's incredible now to think that for a short while I was part of all that old activity. But I stayed in touch with no one.

I've even driven past the bus stop where I used to try to pick up Sheila, on her way to Chiltern Engineering, ahead of her bus. It was still there, still a functioning bus stop. As for the small works itself, I had a little look at that back in the '80s or early '90s, but find that my mind is a blank. Alec Jennings and I remained good friends for years. It's only relatively recently that we've lost touch. But then he would be nearing ninety now. He was twenty-nine when he interviewed me, one of the several people who saved my life when all seemed lost. Also once glanced at from in the car and then forgotten was Custom Refrigeration. If ever a place *deserved* to be forgotten, that was it.

I won't say the same of Power Hydraulics. It's the worst example I have ever seen of what happened to British engineering. There used to be *five* factories on that site. They made aircraft undercarriages, fork-lift trucks, road-surfacing machinery, truck axles, and a number of other products. Every year they took in a large batch of apprentices, while the drawing offices employed dozens of draughtsmen. The workshops were vast, the tradesmen highly skilled. Strikes were non-existent. But it was all wiped out years ago. In its place on that site is a housing estate.

Technical Designs moved on from their offices in the middle of town to a huge, purpose-built new office block in the 1970s. It struck me as too ambitious, even then. Is it still there? I very much doubt it.

And lastly, British Chemicals. The first office block I worked in still stands, together with the associated enormous chemical plant, though nowadays it's under different ownership, and regarded as something of a cash cow, I understand.

But the place where I spent my best years no longer exists in its old form. It was once a prestigious research laboratory, where a number of vitally important discoveries were made in the heyday of the chemical industry before the war. When I first moved in there, with my draughting machine in tow, there were cries of protest from the scientific fraternity. The work I was engaged in wasn't considered pure enough. It lowered the tone rather, they thought.

The last time I looked, that prestigious laboratory had turned into a go-karting arena!

ABOUT THE AUTHOR

Brian Darwent is the author of *Romantic Egotist,* a biography of the writer Jack Trevor Story (of *The Trouble with Harry/ Live Now, Pay Later* fame). Stephen Fry described it as "a wonderful book about an extraordinary and deeply unusual writer and man", George Melly commented that "Brian Darwent has managed the impossible", and Byron Rogers, in a full-page Guardian piece, called it "a little comic classic". He has also been involved in the compiling and editing of several anthologies of William Saroyan's writings, two of them published in America. His own stories and articles appear frequently in small-press literary magazines. He used to earn his living as a draughtsman - long ago, as it now seems.

Available worldwide from Amazon
and all good bookstores

---

www.mtp.agency

www.facebook.com/mtp.agency

@mtp_agency

Michael Terence
Publishing

Printed in Great Britain
by Amazon

40676116R00079